CHASING DAVID

FINDING HOPE AND COURAGE ON THE
TRAIL OF ISRAEL'S GREATEST KING

René Schlaepfer

WITH 8 SMALL GROUP STUDIES

TWIN LAKES CHURCH

APTOS, CA

ISBN 978-1-7331971-0-6

Published by Twin Lakes Press, Aptos California

1st printing: 2019

Unless otherwise indicated, all photographs are by Jamie Rom.

" Rarely have I read a book about a Biblical character that has so moved me to consider fresh angles on a life I thought I knew. With exquisite writing, deep dives into history and a commitment to the humanity of David, René has written a classic. The insights are powerful, soul-shifting and hopeful."

Nancy Ortberg, CEO of Transforming the Bay with Christ

" Chasing David reads part travel guide, part devotional, and part soul-exposing journal. René's scholarship, curiosity, and humor permeate each page. We're taking our whole church through it...this resource is that good!"

Gary L. Gaddini, Lead Pastor, Peninsula Covenant Church

" Some books about biblical characters connect with our mind. Others engage our heart. This book does both with excellence and artistry."

Rev. Dr. Kevin G. Harney, Pastor of Shoreline Community Church and Co-Founder of Organic Outreach International; Author, *Organic Outreach*

" You will never look at David the same way again—and more importantly, you will see yourself and God in a brand new light."

Dan Kimball, Pastor of Vintage Faith Church, author, *The Emerging Church* and *They Like Jesus But Not The Church*

" If you are facing a messy reality, this book will help you find courage for the giants in your life."

Mike Romberger, CEO, Mount Hermon Christian Conference Center

" A unique, creative, engaging resource that draws you into the biblical story in a transformative way. I highly recommend it."

Ken Foreman, Pastor of Cathedral of Faith, author, *Imagine Living Your Dream*

" I learned about David, about myself, and most of all, about the God who delights in me."

Nancy Beach, Leadership Coach, Slingshot Group

" I couldn't put it down."

Karen O'Connor, Award-winning author of more than 75 books, including *Gettin' Old Ain't for Wimps*

" What a book! Sure to energize your faith."

Doug Goodwin, CEO, Kanakuk

" Chasing David is a great adventure!"

Steve Clifford, Pastor, WestGate Church

TO THE READER

This book contains features to enhance its usefulness for groups who use it as curriculum:

- Discussion questions related to each chapter are at the back of the book.

- Video discussion starters filmed in Israel can be found on YouTube by searching for "Chasing David" or at **tlc.org/david**

- Each chapter in the book is divided by Roman numerals into five sections to make it easier if you prefer reading a little portion each weekday as sort of a daily devotional.

I'd encourage you to read the Bible stories in their original settings; the biblical references for the stories are at the start of each chapter.

Let's travel to Israel in these pages. You'll be fascinated by insights from archaeologists and locals we meet along the way. Most importantly, you'll find timeless truths to help you on your own spiritual journey.

CONTENTS

CHASING DAVID

**JULY 23, 1993—THE TEL DAN EXCAVATION
PROJECT, NORTHERN ISRAEL**

It was late afternoon, and light was fading on the partially excavated ruins jutting from the forest floor. The team of archaeologists uncovering a massive city gate from the time of Solomon's temple decided to call it a day. Shadows crept slowly across the ancient paving stones and crumbling walls of the biblical city of Dan as the fierce summer heat began to ease.

Team member Gila Cook took off heavy leather gloves and wiped sweat from her brow with the back of her hand. Then she stopped abruptly.

There was something strange about a rock that had fallen out of a ruined wall she was facing—one side seemed unnaturally flat and polished. She bent down to look more closely at the black basalt. There seemed to be a design etched into its dark surface. She would later explain to reporters that it was only because of the setting sun that she caught a fleeting glimpse of an inscription, the low angle of the light putting the engraved letters into shadowy relief.

She shouted for the team. They ran over and gathered around as Cook, heart pounding, picked up the stone and gently rinsed it with water from her canteen. Sentences carved in neat, clear Aramaic script emerged.

Those who could read the language began to sound out the words.

It was a boast, part of an ancient monument memorializing an military victory over the Israelites. Not far from the bottom of the inscription, the archaeologists saw this:

$$\Delta \mathsf{y} \Delta \mathsf{x} \mathsf{z} \mathsf{9}$$

Reading from right to left, the words were: *Byt Dwd.*

House of David.

The astonished archaeologists realized they were reading something never before seen in any ancient document outside the pages of the Bible, a reference to an empire many had thought was mere myth.

The royal dynasty of David.

✧   ✧   ✧

For three thousand years, King David has captured imaginations.

Classic works of art about David were produced by masters like Michelangelo, Donatello, Rembrandt, and VeggieTales (the part of Bathsheba memorably played by a rubber ducky).

Richard Gere and Gregory Peck starred in films about David, and famed director Ridley Scott is developing a new movie about him.

Songwriter Leonard Cohen's haunting song about David, "Hallelujah," has been recorded by 300 different artists.

Rock superstar Bono says, "At age 12, I was a fan of David. I still am. He was a star, the Elvis of the Bible..."[1]

David's appeal is multicultural: he is an iconic figure in Jewish, Muslim, and Christian scripture. His name is still popular in over 100 languages, from Arabic to Zulu.

David's stories are irresistible: David facing Goliath, David escaping Saul's assassins, David's passion for Bathsheba. His narrative reminds me of thriller writer Raymond Chandler's famous advice to new novelists: "If your story's getting boring, have someone come through the door with a gun." In David's story, there's always someone coming through the door with a gun. Or at least a spear.

David's personality is compelling: other ancient cultures painted their kings as nearly flawless, one-dimensional demigods. Not so with David. As historian Abram Leon Sachar wrote, "He... was cheerful, despondent, selfish, generous, sinning one moment, repenting the next, the most human character of the Bible."[2]

The Bible writers themselves found him endlessly fascinating. He's mentioned by name in the Bible over a thousand times, more than anyone but Jesus. Their narrative of his life, told most colorfully in First and Second Samuel, is riveting. But what makes David unlike any other figure in antiquity is this: those stories are supplemented by song lyrics attributed to David himself, psalms with beautiful turns of phrase that have become part of the world's cultural heritage. So readers not only follow David's story, they feel his feelings and think his thoughts.

And David's importance goes far beyond his own life. God tells him through the prophet Nathan:

> *"I will raise up one of your descendants... I will secure his throne forever. I will be his father, and he will be my son."*
>
> 2 SAMUEL 7:16 NLT

There it is. *The prophecy.* It became what Gerhard Von Rad calls the "undersong" of the Bible, repeated and paraphrased throughout Scripture, understood by both Christians and Jews as a prediction of the Messiah. On this they agree: the Messiah will have David's blood in his veins.[3]

You could say the whole Bible builds up to David. Then looks ahead to the Son of David. In many ways, the Bible is the David/Jesus story.[4]

My personal fascination with the life of David started decades ago as a pastor fresh out of seminary. I grew to love his story so much my wife Laurie and I even named our two sons after David, and David's best friend Jonathan. (Good thing we didn't have more boys; his son's names Shephatiah, Shammua, and Shobab would have been a mouthful, especially when paired with Schlaepfer.)

But as the science of archaeology developed, people fascinated with David had to face an awkward reality: no scholar had ever found physical evidence of David or his empire. At all.

The Bible describes King David as a great ruler over a kingdom that expanded from Egypt to Mesopotamia, the father of a royal dynasty that started around 1000 B.C. and lasted in Jerusalem for hundreds of years. But in modern times many experts doubted his very existence. They saw him as a King Arthur-like myth, a legend crafted to inspire later Jewish refugees.

Their view became known as "biblical minimalism," the idea that the Old Testament consists mostly of fables compiled around 500 B.C., centuries after David. As archaeologist Margreet Steiner wrote:

> When we look for evidence David existed we face an uncomfortable fact. It's not there. No remains of a town, let alone a city, have ever been found. Not a trace. No gate. No houses. Not a single piece... simply nothing.[5]

DAVID'S SECRETS REVEALED

Thanks to discoveries that started at Tel Dan, we now live in a historical moment when that situation is changing.

The piece of polished basalt Gila Cook unearthed there, now in the Israel museum, was part of a much larger monument carved by the king of Damascus about 2,900 years ago to boast of his victory over two enemies: the kingdom of Israel and an empire he calls "The House of David."

Soon after the monument was carved, Israelites recaptured the town and smashed the inscription to pieces. They then (in poetic irony) reused part of the destroyed victory monument to patch a hole in their city walls. That's where it remained hidden for nearly 3,000 years until spotted by Gila Cook.

With this discovery, for the very first time, there was archaeological evidence not only of David but of the fact that he had started a dynasty, a "house."[6] The vast majority of experts today conclude that this inscription proves King David "was a genuine historical figure and not simply the fantastic literary creation of later biblical writers and editors."[7]

TRAIL OF TREASURES

That stone was just the start. More stunning archaeological discoveries related to David followed rapidly, making headlines and creating a trail of long-lost treasures to explore.

But where were the Bible studies that explored David with the help of all these new finds? There were books and videos about traveling in the footsteps of Moses, Jesus, Paul... but not David, arguably the central human figure of the entire Hebrew Scriptures.

So I began to dream of taking a trek like that myself, of writing a Bible study book with a travelogue twist. I longed to bring local color to Old Testament stories that often float without context in a flat flannelgraph neverland.

With all these new discoveries, it was time. This was the moment to go. Thanks to all these finds, we know more about David's era than ever. Now, in a way never before possible, we can chase down the life behind the legend.

You're about to take that trip with me.

RETRACING DAVID'S STEPS

I retraced David's steps in Israel through eight key moments in his life, exploring new excavations, underground caverns, ancient tombs, an oasis in the world's deepest desert, and much more. I traveled with locals who knew the coolest out-of-the-way corners of the country, and with an archaeologist familiar with the latest research. The entire time, I felt like I was putting together a puzzle: with all the new evidence, what was David really like? And what did he *mean*—what was his story, as preserved in the Bible, intended to teach?

I'm coming from my own Christian perspective, but even if you aren't a Christian—or religious at all—there is much here to love. These are timeless tales about living through fear, war, family drama, and divisive political opposition. In an age when all those monsters are on the rampage again, it's time to rediscover David.

His stories will inspire you as they have inspired people for thousands of years—in fact, I'd argue his stories are in some ways even more inspiring today than they have been in many centuries. Because David's world, a strange era lost to history for ages, is being understood with a newfound clarity thanks to those astounding archaeological discoveries and even DNA evidence.

This book is not meant to be *comprehensive* (I won't go verse-by-verse through every biblical story about David), but it is *representative*. I investigated episodes from each major phase of his life.

WARNING: UNCOMFORTABLE TRUTH AHEAD

But here's a warning: I won't hold back the unsavory aspects of David's character. Centuries of Sunday School sanitizing have reduced David to a plucky character who brought down a giant (or, in the case of VeggieTales, a giant pickle). He has become a meme about the little guy winning. The David of the Bible is much more real—and adult—than that.

In fact, his stories are so rough, so raw, they seem deliberately designed to provoke debate. In David's story, neat theology meets messy reality. One question David is guaranteed to raise every time anyone reads deeper than the Children's Bible stories: "How is this crusty, inconsistent character a 'man after God's own heart,' as the Bible describes him?"

It's really one of the ultimate mysteries of the Bible: Why is the *entire Bible* written this way, with so many flawed people doing so many stupid things—David perhaps the most extreme example?

One of the biggest surprises for people reading the Bible for the first time is that it's not the simplistic propaganda many assume it will be. There's rarely a moral at the end of each story. The heroes aren't always heroic. The saints aren't super saintly. Yes, there are commandments... which no one ever completely keeps.

So why all the soap opera? What's it all mean?

I believe there's a single, unifying, over-arching theme to these stories that we often miss, and it's particularly important to understanding David. Get David's story right and you'll understand the meaning behind every other story in the Bible.

❈ ❈ ❈

What I discovered on my journey completely changed the way I look at David.

And along the way, something else happened. This trip impacted not only the way I understand David, but the way I understand myself.

As I prepared for this book, I found myself in a deep emotional trough, the darkest since my early days in ministry. I was wrestling with profound self-doubt.

I am the Senior Pastor of a church that is, by most measures, healthy and vibrant—a warm and generous congregation in a place of world-class beauty, the Monterey Bay of California. My wife and three 20-something children are loving people of great character.

Yet I wondered almost daily if anything I'd accomplished as a pastor really made any difference. And how could God use someone like me anyway, so inconsistent, so weak? I was tired. Frustrated. Unconvinced of my competence to handle the challenges of my job. I'd read that Walt Disney once took an extended break from his studio because he had what he described as "...a bad case of the DDs: disillusionment and discouragement."[8] That's exactly how I felt.

So in the middle of this emotional battle, I boarded a plane in San Francisco with Laurie and our friend Jamie Rom, this project's photographer. Destination: Israel. I hoped to trace David's trail and discover new insights into his story. And as I stared out the plane window and watched the Bay Area recede, I breathed a silent prayer.

God, let me find something that will help me hang in there too. ✻

DIGGING DEEPER

THE MOABITE STONE

When French historian Andre Lemaire saw reports of the Tel Dan discovery, a faint bell rang in his memory. Where had he seen something like this before? His hunch led him into the depths of the Louvre museum in Paris where he studied an artifact that had been stored there for 125 years—the Moabite Stone, also known as the Mesha Stele.

Discovered in Jordan in 1868 by Anglican missionary and amateur archaeologist Frederick Augustus Klein, this ancient monument was inscribed around 840 B.C. by King Mesha of Moab. Scholars had long known the Moabite Stone contained the oldest reference outside the Bible to *Yahweh*, the God of Israel.

But Lemaire thought he recalled one obscure line that had escaped scholarly attention. He examined the inscription with his magnifying glass... and found it. In line 31. A reference to "The House of David." No one had noticed it before because, at the time of the Moabite Stone's discovery, understanding of its ancient language was still in its infancy. Many archaeologists today, including Lemaire, support the view that this is another ancient reference to David and his dynasty.[9]

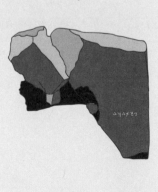

ONE

FINDING CONFIDENCE WHEN REJECTED

1 SAMUEL 16

I

DAVID'S POST-APOCALYPTIC WORLD

It's early in the morning on my first day in Israel's capital. Jet lag has kicked in, and I'm staring at the ceiling of my room, unable to sleep. After pouring a quick cup of coffee I decide to throw on some clothes and take a stroll.

The city is just waking up, shopkeepers sweeping away the night debris from the sidewalks, a few taxis prowling the streets looking for late partiers or early commuters. As I sip my coffee and take it all in, a pattern quickly becomes apparent.

I amble down King David Avenue. Past the King David Hotel. The David Citadel Hotel. The King David Residence Hotel. The Tower of David. David's Jewelry Shop. Even the David Falafel Restaurant. More than 3,000 years after he made this city his capital, David still captures imaginations here in Jerusalem, now known as "David's City."

Yet when David was born, this was all still enemy territory. In fact, the first time Jerusalem residents ever saw David, they mocked him from the walls of their fortress.

But I'm getting ahead of myself. To understand David I need to start at square one.

Bethlehem.

When David was born, the world was exploding.

The date: Circa 1040 B.C.

The event: The tail end of the most disruptive social change in human history, what historians call the Late Bronze Age Collapse. This was a period of about 300 years even more catastrophic than the European Dark Ages or the fall of the Roman Empire.

The mystery: Around 1200 B.C., almost all the kingdoms in the Mediterranean and the Fertile Crescent, which had been enjoying a long Golden Age, began to rapidly collapse. Some never recovered. No one knows exactly why. There is evidence of severe famine, volcanic eruption, earthquakes, and roaming bands of pirates, all happening at once.

Whatever the reason, advanced empires that had flourished for centuries came to an abrupt end. Entire languages were lost. Technologies disappeared. That led to about 300 years of post-apocalyptic anarchy, when small bands of people did their best to survive.

I can't emphasize enough how important it is to read the biblical stories of this era (the Book of Judges and the early monarchy) in this context. It was a time of complete social upheaval, violence often necessary to escape extinction.

The closest thing to this in our contemporary imaginations, as strange as the analogy may sound, is the zombie apocalypse movie genre, with outnumbered survivors forging small alliances against an overwhelming and super-powered foe.

Except that, during the Late Bronze Age Collapse, the role of the zombies was played by a mysterious group known as the "Sea Peoples," warriors who frightened even the strongest kings as they roamed the world causing chaos and destruction.

The Sea Peoples left no monuments or written records of their own. Everything historians know about them comes from letters and inscriptions created by those who tried to resist them—and all those references are soaked in fear.[1]

"They came from the sea in their warships and none could stand against them," warns one inscription written in the 13th century B.C. and later found at the Egyptian city of Tanis. "They desolated our people and land," reads another.[2]

So who were the Sea Peoples? An inscription in the mortuary temple of Pharaoh Ramses III describes them as an amalgam of tribes including "the Peleset." Scholars are still unsure exactly who all these groups were. But many theorize that the "Peleset" are the Philistines of the Bible.

The opportunity: The weakening of the superpower states was also an opening for smaller groups of people. With no larger empire dominating the region, it was the perfect time for the loose coalition of Israelite tribes to band together and form a kingdom. This was their big chance.

The problem: There was another band of people also hoping to scratch out their own kingdom in the same territory. Bigger problem: They were the Philistines.

Technologically, artistically, and militarily the Philistines were far more advanced than the Israelites. They were experienced fighters from a warrior culture. How could the Israelites possibly hope to counter this feared foe? They tried rallying their fiercely independent tribal families around a unifying king. But the first Israelite king, Saul, proved unable and unstable as a leader—inconsistent, self-absorbed, and disobedient.

As David's story begins, the prophet Samuel, who had revealed Saul years before as the one chosen to lead the nation, boldly proclaims that God has rejected him as king. To find the next monarch, God directs Samuel to a town called Bethlehem.

✧   ✧   ✧

After my pre-dawn stroll, I hail a cab to travel to Bethlehem. It's only six miles from Jerusalem, but to get there visitors have to go through a high-security border checkpoint at a concrete wall topped with barbed wire. Some say the wall is necessary for security. Others say it's an overreaction that has caused pain for many innocent people.

While waiting in the long line of traffic I try to strip away the cement and graffiti in front of me and imagine the Bethlehem of David's day.

Of course I'm picturing all the Christmas carols, greeting cards, and nativity plays set here. Bethlehem? As in, "O Little

Town of...”? I've heard about it my whole life. In ancient times it was small. Overlooked. Out of the way. David was born poor, in a poor town.

I would soon learn that most of what I thought I knew about this place was wrong. Archaeologists have recently unearthed strange underground crypts that change our picture of ancient Bethlehem completely.

✧　　✧　　✧

The taxi drops me off near Manger Square, the famous center of the city, where I've arranged to meet a local guide. I arrive a little early, so I take some time to look around.

Then something magical happens.

I find myself drawn by an amazing aroma, something like freshly baked bread—only much more intense. I spot a wooden wagon loaded with what looks like foot-long oval-shaped pretzels steaming in the morning light. I put my face in the steam. And I smell one of the most delicious smells I have ever smelled in a lifetime of smelling.

This is my introduction to a new culinary love for life—the “Jerusalem bagel.” These amazing concoctions bear almost no resemblance to their dense American-style cousins. They're long and soft and crusted with sesame seeds, and at this early time of day they're fresh, hot out of the oven. I buy one and sink my teeth into its wheaty softness. My eyes roll back in my head. Gluten nirvana.

Why mention it here? A similar aroma must have filled this place in David's time, because the word Bethlehem literally means “House of Bread.” It probably got its name because it's one of the only areas in the ancient Israelite hill country with a few narrow valleys flat enough for grain cultivation—and water abundant enough for year-round irrigation. No wonder the bread here is so good. The tradition goes back centuries! That adds a little sensory depth as you imagine David's story. He came from "Breadtown."

Incidentally, one of the ways archaeologists can tell they're excavating an Israelite city and not, say, a Philistine city, is the presence of distinctly Israelite-style bread-baking trays. Ancient Israelites *loved* baking. They left evidence everywhere in the form of round pizza-type trays, totally unknown in Philistine culture. One way to know if a ruin is Israelite? Look for the baking trays!

I'm seriously contemplating whether I should buy a third Jerusalem bagel when the local guide I've hired for the day walks up, a poised woman in her mid-40s named Sara, with long black hair, piercing blue eyes, and regal bearing. I reluctantly tear myself away from the bread cart and we exchange greetings. I try to make a good impression with my big American-style smile and a firm handshake. She smiles back, and with elegance and grace points out that I've got several stubborn sesame seeds stuck in my teeth.

DIGGING DEEPER

IT'S THE WATER, AND A LOT MORE

Bethlehem is one of the oldest human settlements, its origins going back to prehistoric times.

Scholars believe the original settlers of Bethlehem were nomads who discovered that if they stayed in this one spot they could have everything they needed. There's grass to feed goats, fertile hills to grow almonds (probably the first trees cultivated by humans); gentle slopes for olive trees (their oil used for fuel, cooking, and soap), valleys to grow grain, large caves for homes. This settled lifestyle gave these early Bethlehem residents leisure time to create some of the first art. The earliest carving of a human couple yet found is in a cave nearby.[3]

The land here is so fertile because Bethlehem sits on an enormous aquifer that waters the fields even in summer. To this day, the best tasting water in the whole region of Judea is said to come from Bethlehem. This helps explain a strange episode in 2 Samuel 23. David longs for a drink from the wells of Bethlehem, then in enemy hands. So three of his buddies sneak behind battle lines to get it for him. Having now sampled Israel's water myself, which ranges from sulfurous well water to Bethlehem's amazing spring water, I get it. The water here is still the best.

✳

As we walk through the ancient Church of the Nativity—built above the cave that is the traditional birthplace of Jesus Christ—Sara tells me that her family, like many here in Bethlehem, traces its local roots all the way back to Bible times. Three thousand years ago her ancestors may have worked in the very hills and valleys where David watched sheep and wrote psalms. I tell her how a hundred years ago my ancestors were lumberjacks near Zurich. Sara is unimpressed.

After I explain that I'm trying to follow the historic trail of David, she says she knows just where to begin.

We get into a cab, headed to a field just outside town.

On our drive, Sara tells me of a spectacular discovery made nearby just a few years ago.

SECRET CHAMBERS OF THE DEAD

While building an industrial park near Bethlehem in 2013, bulldozer operators accidentally uncovered two deep holes leading to subterranean chambers that had been sealed and forgotten for over 2,000 years. The Israeli government has an emergency response team for just such discoveries, part of the Israeli Antiquities Authority. A team of IAA researchers sped to the site, dropped into the holes, and snapped on their flashlights. They were amazed to find a massive 7.4-acre underground necropolis (literally, "city of the dead,") with at least 100 lavish tombs. For the next two years archaeologists explored and mapped these vast caverns.

The crypts they found date from about 2000 B.C. to about 650 B.C.. So the time of David's birth (around 1040 B.C.) would have been right in the heart of activity at this necropolis. The many jars, bowls, lamps, and bronze objects found inside imply a nearby city sophisticated and large enough to provide sacred objects for these tombs.[4]

Scholars say this means that, in David's time, Bethlehem was not a tiny, poor, unknown village in the middle of nowhere. It was an important sacred burial site for those of wealth and power, a prestigious place with the best artisans, located directly on a strategic north-south trade route. Picture a modern place of religious pilgrimage and you'll get an idea of its importance and wealth.

PUZZLES SOLVED

The necropolis may help explain some puzzling details in the Bible, like why, centuries before David, the patriarch Joseph buried his beloved wife Rachel here instead of in the family tomb in Hebron. It probably wasn't just that she died here; Hebron is only a few miles away. She may have been entombed here because this was already a prestigious burial ground.

It also helps explain the prophet Samuel's strange cover story. When Samuel visits Bethlehem to find a new king, he has to hide his purpose from the king's agents—his actual agenda, had it been known, would have gotten him killed. So, the Bible says, he puts a rope around a cow's neck and explains to any curious onlookers that he is simply journeying to make a sacrifice there.

That has always seemed like a very bizarre ruse to me (to avoid being noticed, you're going to walk into town leading a cow on a leash?) but these new discoveries help explain that strange detail. Now that we know Bethlehem was a holy site, the story makes sense; the people here probably saw many visitors regularly offering prayers and sacrifices to honor the dead.

DIGGING DEEPER

O BIG TOWN?

If archaeology demonstrates that Bethlehem was a prosperous, sophisticated city, doesn't that contradict the Bible—not to mention generations of Christmas carols? We think of it as the "little town" we sing about every December. And in Micah 5:2, Bethlehem is called "the least of the towns of Judah."

The newly discovered tombs actually synchronize perfectly with Bible history. The lavish burials near Bethlehem stopped abruptly in the year 650 B.C. That's also around the time the name "Bethlehem" stops appearing in literary sources. Not until the birth of Jesus Christ is Bethlehem mentioned again in any ancient documents. What happened?

The Assyrians and Babylonians were invading Israel and Judah at that time, their armies apparently beating Bethlehem into a near-oblivion that lasted centuries. The Book of Micah was written at the start of this steep decline of the once-prosperous town. When Jesus was born, Bethlehem was just beginning to revive from those devastating wars.

✻

The cab lets us out at a quiet suburban street. Sara leads me through a church gate and past several crowded outdoor shrines, to a cliff overlooking the field that for centuries has been traditionally identified as the ancestral land of Boaz, David's great-grandfather. If David's father Jesse inherited this property, then he would have been a wealthy man. Somehow the field has escaped most modern development. As they have for thousands of years, shepherds still tend sheep there.

Sara and I walk further, down a hillside to a small cave. She tells me Bethlehem locals treasure this spot as an unspoiled corner of their famous town.

Bending over to peer inside, I see an ancient manger made of stone, evidence shepherds have used this as a makeshift barn for centuries. I stand in the cave entrance, smelling the grit, the manure, and the hay, and imagine the humble beginnings of Israel's greatest king.

II
GOD'S UNEXPECTED CHOICE

The prophet Samuel was clearly regarded as a mysterious and somewhat dangerous figure. As he approaches Bethlehem, the town's alarmed elders meet him outside the city and ask his intentions. He assures them he comes in peace and invites the elders—and Jesse—to join him at the sacrificial ritual. When everyone is assembled, he turns to Jesse and makes a surprising request.

"Bring all your sons before me," Samuel commands. One of them is about to be chosen as the new ruler of the Israelites.

Samuel must have been imagining the sort of person God would select. King Saul is described in Scripture as tall and powerful. So Samuel's probably picturing someone who can out-tall and out-power Saul. A younger upgrade, Saul 2.0.

What happens instead takes him completely by surprise.

LEFT OUT

Several young men line up before Samuel. He looks up at the strapping oldest son, Eliab, and thinks, "Wow, this guy is impressive, must be God's choice." But God says:

> "*Do not consider his appearance or his height, for I have rejected him. The LORD does not look at the things people look at. People look at the outward appearance, but the LORD looks at the heart.*"
>
> 1 SAMUEL 16:7 NIV

When translated directly from the original Hebrew that last phrase literally reads, "*Man sees face. God sees heart.*" So Samuel passes on son number one. And the next one. And the next, and the next, and the next, and the next, all the way down the line, until he runs out of sons. Finally Samuel asks Jesse, "Are these all the sons you have?" Jesse's answer is very telling. Well...

> "*There is still the youngest, but he is out in the fields watching the sheep and goats.*"
>
> 1 SAMUEL 16:11 NLT

I'm not the first person to wonder why you'd leave one of your sons out of the loop when a famed kingmaker asks to see them all. And notice how Jesse doesn't even call David by name. He just says, "the youngest." In Hebrew, the word is *haqqaton*. It can mean "the baby." Some suggest it even implies "the runt." The same word was used for a pinky finger. *Haqqaton*. "Well, there's pinky."

Samuel seems a little angry when he barks, "Send for him—immediately!" To heighten the sense of urgency he feels the need to add, "No one is sitting down, and no one is eating a thing, until he gets here!"

And of course it turns out—he's the one. God chooses the family runt.

FAMILY PROBLEMS

I think there's evidence in the Bible beyond this story that David did not have the most positive family-of-origin experience. In the next chapter, David's brother Eliab says to David:

> *"I know how conceited you are and how wicked your heart is!"*
>
> 1 SAMUEL 17:28 NIV

Not a huge fan of baby brother. Later in Psalm 69:8 David writes, "Even my own brothers pretend they don't know me; they treat me like a stranger."

There's something else that makes David a very unlikely candidate for king. His great-grandmother, Ruth, was a refugee from Moab. The Moabites at one time were absolutely the most despised minority group in Israel. Deuteronomy 23:3 says, "No Moabite or any of his descendants may enter the assembly of the Lord, even down to the tenth generation."

But none of that stops God from choosing David. When David finally arrives, young, dirty, smelling like sheep, God tells Samuel:

> *"Rise and anoint him; he is the one."*
>
> 1 SAMUEL 16:12 NIV

Samuel takes the special oil he has brought with him and pours it on David's head.

This wasn't just your common kitchen-cabinet olive oil. The precise recipe for Israelite anointing oil is preserved in the Book of Exodus (Exod. 20:22–25). The finest olive oil was blended with myrrh, cinnamon, cassia (a tree bark similar to cinnamon), and aromatic cane (which smells something like ginger). This fragrant mixture was used to anoint, or set apart, individuals for special service. In this case it was sort of a pre-coronation ceremony, designating David as the future king. He is the anointed one. (The Hebrew word for "the anointed one" is *mashiach*, which English Bibles often render as Messiah.)

And God not only chooses David; he *empowers* David with the Holy Spirit.

> *And the Spirit of the LORD came powerfully upon David from that day on.*
>
> 1 SAMUEL 16:13 NIV

So David is God's unexpected choice. And here is precisely where many books and sermons about David begin to go wrong.

III
THE MAN AFTER GOD'S OWN HEART

I've heard a lot of preachers do a lot of guesswork about the reasons God must have chosen David.

He had proven himself loyal by tending sheep.

Shown himself brave by defeating lions.

Demonstrated his heart for God by composing worship songs out in the fields at night.

So, they add, if you want God to choose you too, then that is how you should live. Be loyal, brave, devout.

Great advice. Problem is, none of that is in the text. This story does not seem to be about how David somehow *earned* God's blessing. The point is apparently that God simply *picked* him. When no one else did.

Even the famous verse that calls David "a man after God's own heart" (1 Samuel 13:14) has some interesting shades of meaning. My friend Sandra Richter has a PhD in the Hebrew Bible from Harvard and many years of experience on archaeological excavations in Israel. She's also the author of several books on the Old Testament and the Chair of Biblical Studies at Westmont College.

She points out that the text reflects an ancient saying that has to do with the *choice of a monarch*. That David is a "man after God's heart" means David is God's choice, a man God's heart has gone after.

> Although most interpret this phrase to mean that David
> had a particularly keen affection for Yahweh or that
> David had bent his will after Yahweh's, in reality, this text
> reflects an Akkadian idiom that has to do with the choice
> of a suzerain. Yahweh has... chosen David because David
> is (in Hebrew)... "a man according to his heart." In other
> words, David is "a king of God's choosing."[5]

That helps explain so much! It's not just a verse about David's heart; it's a verse about God's heart. His heart went after David.

NAMED BELOVED

I imagine David's memory of this moment stayed vivid for the rest of his life: the powerful voice of Samuel, the rich cinnamon-ginger smell of the special oil, the viscous feel of it as it oozes over his forehead and across his eyelids and down his neck, and, after he opens his eyes, the stunned looks on the faces of his brothers and father. This moment of anointing will carry him through some of his darkest days. He stays thrilled at his *chosenness* even decades later:

> *"Who am I, O Sovereign LORD... that you have brought me this far? ... What more can I say to you? You know what your servant is really like, Sovereign LORD."*
>
> 2 SAMUEL 7:18,20 NLT

David's very name means *"beloved,"* and although it seems he did not always receive "beloved" treatment from his own family, for the rest of his life David finds security and joy in the fact that he is beloved by God.

This does not prevent him from moral failure. But it does keep drawing him back to health, back to life, back to God—even after he makes serious, destructive mistakes. David is at his best when he leans into his anointing.

YOU ARE CHOSEN TOO

This is a theme that runs all through the Bible. All the way down to you and me.

As the New Testament reiterates again and again, our motivation to live righteously is not so that God will choose us; it's that God has *already* chosen us in Christ. David's experience is just one story to show how God always works.

A thousand years after David, the Apostle Paul wrote these words to a Corinthian church full of the sort of people least likely to be selected for any kind of honor:

Few of you were wise in the world's eyes or powerful or wealthy when God called you. But God chose the foolish things of the world to shame the wise; God chose the weak things of the world to shame the strong... God chose the lowly things of this world and the despised things—and the things that are not—to nullify the things that are, so that no one may boast before him.

1 CORINTHIANS 1:26B–29 NIV

Humans tend to have an unspoken point system based on looks or wealth or talent or coolness or ability. But their point system means nothing to God. He sees you through his grace and his grace alone.

> David's experience is just one story to show how God always works.

BLESSINGS POURED ON YOU

Did that ancient recipe for the sacred anointing oil used by Samuel seem rich and fragrant? It's nothing compared to what God pours on you. The Bible has a word for it: Grace.

Paul takes a whole chapter in his letter to the Ephesians to describe it. Look at some of these ingredients:

God... has blessed us with every spiritual blessing in the heavenly realms because we are united with Christ. Even before he made the world, God loved us and chose us in Christ to be holy and without fault in his eyes... So we praise God for the glorious grace he has poured out on us who belong to his dear Son.

And God not only *chose* you, he *empowered* you with the Holy Spirit, just as he did for David:

When you believed in Christ, he identified you as his own by giving you the Holy Spirit, whom he promised long ago.

Why would God choose you? For a simple yet astonishing reason:

This is what he wanted to do, and it gave him great pleasure.

Keep reminding yourself of that truth. When others put you down—when you put yourself down—keep preaching the gospel to yourself. God loved you and chose you and empowered you. Not because of anything you did to earn it, not because you proved yourself worthy, not because you are better than anyone else, but just because *he wanted to do it*, and it *gave him pleasure!*

GOD'S CHOICE

Brennan Manning was a disciplined man who strove to improve himself. At various points in his life he was a Marine, a Franciscan priest, a hermit in a remote desert cave, and a mason's assistant in France—his earnest efforts at self-improvement sometimes undermined by his alcoholism. He wrote about how, after much frustration, he eventually came to realize that although he had been trying to earn God's approval through his behavior, this is not why God chooses to love:

> ...unlike ourselves, the God and Father of Jesus loves men and women not for what he finds in them, but for what he finds in himself. It is not because men and women are good that he loves them, nor only good men and women that he loves. It's because he is so unspeakably, unutterably, unimaginably good, that God loves all men and women— even sinners. He does not detect what is congenial, attractive and appealing, and then respond to it with his favor... He initiates love... his love is creative, it originates good rather than rewarding it. That's why St. Augustine can write those lyrical lines, "In loving me, you made me lovable."[6]

David did not do something to merit God's attention and affection. God chose him simply because he determined to choose him.

IV
RELAXING IN YOUR CHOSENNESS

Maybe you too, like David, come from a very humble background.

Maybe you, like David, have a history of mistreatment from your own family.

Maybe, like him, you are from a minority group looked down on historically in your culture.

Maybe no one saw anything great in you either. You were sized up and left out, picked on and written off.

None of that stops God.

God sees you, with your wounds, your shortcomings, your embarrassments, and He whispers, "*I choose you. I empower you. You have a role in my plan for the world.*"

WHAT VOICE ARE YOU LISTENING TO?

You may not hear the voices of family dismissing you as unqualified or unlovable; you may hear that from yourself, the critical voice in your own head. You may call yourself names you'd never call anyone else.

> God sees you, with your wounds, your shortcomings, your embarrassments, and He whispers, "*I choose you.*"

"*Stupid, stupid, stupid...*"

Listen instead to God whispering to you. In a way, he gives David's name to all of us. Do you hear it?

"*Beloved, beloved, beloved, beloved...*"

I like the way Martyn Lloyd-Jones puts it:

Have you realized that much of your unhappiness in life is due to the fact that you are listening to yourself instead of talking to yourself? Take those thoughts that come to you the moment you wake up in the morning. You have not originated them but they are talking to you, they bring

back the problems of yesterday, etc. Say, "Self, listen for a
moment, I will speak to you."[7]

Talk back to those thoughts. Replace their critical voices
with what God says about you, according to Scripture. You are
chosen. Beloved. Empowered.

DESTINY FROM DAY ONE

Perhaps you still feel unworthy to be chosen by God. You feel you
don't deserve it. You haven't done enough. You haven't earned it.

But notice this: David sees that, though he first learned of
God's choice at the moment of his physical anointing, really God
had chosen him and given him a destiny long before he could do
anything to deserve it. In Psalm 139, David writes:

> *You made all the delicate, inner parts of my body*
> *and knit me together in my mother's womb.*
> *Thank you for making me so wonderfully complex!*
> *Your workmanship is marvelous—how well I know it.*
> *You watched me as I was being formed in utter seclusion,*
> *as I was woven together in the dark of the womb.*
> *You saw me before I was born.*
> *Every day of my life was recorded in your book.*
> *Every moment was laid out*
> *before a single day had passed.*
>
> PSALM 139:13–16 NLT

When you read these verses in light of the fact that David's
own father didn't consider him worthy of Samuel's attention, they
have extra resonance.

David is saying, no matter the circumstances of my birth and childhood, I will find my identity in this: Long before I could do anything right, long before I could do anything wrong, while still in the womb unable to earn anything or deserve anything, God was with me, and God had a plan for me!

✣　✣　✣

Christian counselor David Seamands writes about what those verses meant to a woman named Betty. Her parents felt forced to marry because her mother was pregnant with her. It was an undesired marriage and Betty was an undesired child. When Betty was three and a half, her father left. She carried the sense of being an unwanted accident with her for most of her life. Then one day at the end of a counseling session Dr. Seamands gave her some homework based on these verses in Psalm 139.

He said, "I want you to imagine the very moment of your conception... As you think about that, ask yourself one question, *Where was God at that moment?*"

When they met a week later, Betty told him that at first she thought the whole assignment was crazy. But about the third day, when she really concentrated on it, she began to cry. Then she wrote down this prayer in her journal:

> O God, *my heart leaps with the thought that you, my loving father, have never forsaken me. You were there when I was conceived... You looked upon me with a father's love even then. You were thinking of me in my mother's womb, molding me... You were there when my mother gave birth to me, standing in the vacant place of my father. You were there when I cried the bitter tears of*

a child whose father has abandoned her. You were holding me in your gentle arms all the while, rocking me gently in your soothing love... God, my dear, dear Father, my heart had turned to frost, but the light of your love is beginning to warm it.[8]

START WITH GOD-ESTEEM, NOT SELF-ESTEEM

When you speak truth to those critical voices, make sure you get this detail right: David's story is not about how other people perceived him as young, small, and unqualified, yet were proven *wrong*. At the time, he *was* young and small and unqualified. But he wasn't *just* that. He was also *chosen*.

If you tell yourself, "No matter what people say, I am not unqualified, I am not weak," it doesn't usually

You are chosen.
You are beloved.
You are empowered.

work for long because deep down you know the truth: there are indeed situations where you are weak and unqualified. So remind yourself of God's empowering grace.

As Brennan Manning puts it:

> *...Grace calls out, "You are not just a disillusioned old man who may die soon, a middle-aged woman stuck in a job and desperately wanting to get out, a young person feeling the fire in the belly begin to grow cold. You may be insecure, inadequate, mistaken or potbellied. Death, panic, depression, and disillusionment may be near you. But you are not just that. You are accepted." Never confuse your perception of yourself with the mystery that you really are accepted.*[9]

V
YOUR MISSION

Standing in that Bethlehem cave, I'm struck by a parallel between David's era and ours. Just as David started his life in a time of chaos and transition during the Late Bronze Age Collapse, it can feel like our world is in chaos too. Long-standing institutions are under threat. People seem more divided than ever. Tribe battles tribe. Fear runs rampant.

Some respond by retreating into caves like this—ever-smaller places of supposed safety. Instead, we need to consider ourselves deputized by God as David was. We have a mission. Jesus said we're the light of the world!

But as we prepare to go out into that threatening environment, we must first receive and believe in God's anointing—the grace and power he pours on our lives.

Because you will meet opposition. You will hear criticism, insults, and threats. That's why it's crucial to make the foundation of your identity how *God* sees you, not how *others* see you. And that's something you can only *receive*, not *achieve*.

✧　　✧　　✧

The extended time in this manger-cave on the outskirts of Bethlehem has been rich. I thank Sara as we prepare to part.

"I found myself deeply moved here."

"I'm so glad," she says.

"You seem moved yourself, like there's something you want to say."

"Well, yes." She hesitates. "There's still one little sesame seed stuck in your teeth."

As my taxi rolls through Bethlehem's streets and I try to pry out the stubborn seed with the edge of Sara's business card, it occurs to me that, although David is chosen, he does not coast his way into the kingdom.

He is chosen. He is *going* to be king. That is his God-given destiny. Yet between here and there, he will encounter steep hills and dark valleys. David will face battles and betrayals, slipups and successes, lush palaces and dark caverns, fan worship and assassination attempts. How does he get through it all?

You'll see him continually point his thoughts back to *this moment*, the time he first realized, *I am chosen.* He keeps reminding himself, *I have a destiny.*

Your chosenness does not mean life will be struggle-free for you either. Yes, you have a destiny; yes, you are beloved by God. But there are valleys to endure and hills to climb for you too.

> Your chosenness does not mean life will be struggle-free.

When bad things happen to you, that does not mean God has *un-chosen* you. It just means life is happening. Remind yourself of your own *chosenness.* And watch how God redeems even the detours, delays, and disasters to accomplish your destiny.

THOUGHT EXPERIMENT

Time for me to practice what I preach.

Back in the hotel I realize how, in the months before my trip, I'd been focusing almost entirely on my performance—as a pastor, husband, father, friend. And generally feeling like a failure.

But today I was reminded that my chosenness before God is not based on my performance. It's based on God's will.

So I decide to try a thought experiment. For at least the duration of this journey, I will actively choose to see myself as chosen, as someone with a destiny from God. And I will choose to see whatever happens every day as something God can use for purpose.

Please don't get me wrong. I believe in a multi-pronged approach to attack discouragement: exercise, diet, counseling, research, support, and meds, if necessary. But I'm starting to see that for me, the core of the cure is a kind of spiritual cognitive therapy: I need to honestly analyze my thinking and redirect it, not just get lazy and let the dour thoughts cascade over my brain like some lukewarm waterfall. To mix metaphors, I need to inhale the fragrance of the anointing oil that God so lavishly pours on me.

You see David doing this through his life. He continually fortifies himself with reminders of what happened on this day in Bethlehem. The day he was told he was chosen. And he believed it.

He will need every bit of that belief when he sees the giant warrior waiting for him just over the horizon. ✵

DIGGING DEEPER

BEER ARCHAEOLOGY

If the ancient Israelites loved making their grain into bread, does that mean they enjoyed the other ancient grain product... beer? Ask the beer archaeologists. Yes, there is such a thing.

In 2019, a team of Israeli researchers used 3,000-year-old yeast and other trace ingredients found in pottery vessels at archaeological sites in Israel to recreate the beer that David may have quaffed.

It's actually serious science. In a long-term, multi-disciplinary research project, scientists captured yeast that was still alive yet dormant from beer cups found at excavations in Tel Aviv, Gath, Jerusalem, and the Negev Desert. They isolated six different strains of yeast that were still viable after thousands of years underground. Using DNA sequencing, they were able to recreate the six unique beers those vessels once held. One scientist compared the process to the recreation of dinosaurs in Jurassic Park.[10]

They are now looking for funding to begin marketing the beers to the general public. Because we live in a fallen world, I guarantee you that right now someone, somewhere, is thinking of branding it "HeBrews."

✱

TWO

FINDING COURAGE TO FACE GIANTS

I
THE VALLEY OF ELAH

Imagine the shouts. They echo from a valley shaped like a massive oval sports stadium, large enough to hold over 200,000 people. Onlookers throng the surrounding hills, watching as two combatants approach each other, circling, trash-talking at an epic level. In moments one will die.

This is the Elah Valley in Israel, where one of the most famous fights in history went down. Three thousand years ago, an Israelite shepherd boy vanquished the Philistine giant Goliath here, changing his country's history—forever.

At least, that's what I learned in Sunday School.

But how much of this story is fiction and how much is fact? Is there any evidence outside the Bible that this confrontation ever occurred? Why is this strange story even in the Bible?

Just a month before I traveled to Israel on my David quest, I was still wrestling with how to approach this. I knew it would be the greatest challenge I'd face in this entire project: How could I write in a fresh way about something most people think they already know—and either consider a nice but overly familiar Sunday School story, or dismiss as pure fairy tale?

It's the drama almost everyone links with David, a tale so woven into the fabric of our culture that it has the status of an iconic myth. The term "David vs. Goliath" has been used thousands of times to describe battles in the sports, legal, and business worlds.

But while many appreciate its power as parable, they hesitate to call it history. Some academics question whether the Israelites even existed as described in this story, with an organized kingdom and army. If I'm going on the trail of David, I have to ask myself, *Does the evidence truly direct me to a real place here in Israel—or into the realm of fantasy?*

As my trip approached, I searched scholarly papers, popular books, even TED talks and web sites on the subject. I was looking for any legit archaeology that might shed light on the David and Goliath story.

As usual when surfing the Internet I found lots of weird garbage (did you know Goliath was from a race of alien giants who built Atlantis?), but one name popped up again and again on TV programs and web sites and magazine articles— archaeologist Danny Herman. He's been interviewed by PBS America, the Smithsonian Channel, and many others. A professor at Hebrew University, he's an expert on biblical archaeology. He's led tours for celebrities like Dr. Oz, plus execs from GoDaddy, Google, Apple, Samsung, and several Nobel Prize winners. So I took a chance and emailed him. "Can I interview you about David and Goliath?"

He responded within hours. Not only did he agree to an interview, he offered to drive me, my wife, and our project videographer to a site where he said exciting discoveries related to this story have recently been made—and to be our guide through much of the rest of my David journey. "I want to make it clear," he writes, "I am not going to show you the headless skeleton of a giant. But what we have is compelling evidence for the environment in which the battle may have happened—and the era in which David lived."

✧   ✧   ✧

One month later, we roll into the driveway of Danny's house about 20 minutes west of Jerusalem. I ring the doorbell and he wrenches it open, grins, and shouts, "Shalom!" A wiry, spectacled man in his mid-40s, Danny bursts with enthusiasm for his family, his country, his field of study. In fact he's pretty much enthusiastic about everything. If his comments were visible as texts they'd have lots of thumbs-up and wide-eye emojis. He quickly helps us transfer our gear to his four-wheel drive. "We're off!" he proclaims as he slams his Jeep into gear and roars away, rocketing us southward over the rolling hills to the Elah Valley.

On the way I decide to cut to the chase and ask a simple question. "Danny, I've read quotes from several scholars who claim there's no evidence whatsoever for David or the Davidic empire—"

He jumps in before I can finish. "Who are you reading? This situation is definitely changing!" He launches into an impromptu lecture as if I were one of his university students, often turning toward me to see if I agree while the car hurtles ahead at breakneck speeds. I find myself agreeing quickly and often.

Soon we roll into the Elah Valley. It's early spring after a very wet winter, so wildflowers are abundant, blood-red poppies and yellow mustard plants sprinkled everywhere on the brilliant green hillsides. A modern two-lane highway bisects the valley, but Danny slows down, looking for something.

"Where are you—" I start to ask, and suddenly we veer off the road and plunge into a field. Bouncing over rocks and skidding through puddles, Danny steers his four-wheeler straight up a hill. When we lurch to a stop, he announces we're facing one of the most astounding archaeological discoveries of our century.

These are the ruins of Khirbet Qeiyafa.

✧   ✧   ✧

Archaeological thrillers abound with stories of ancient lost cities, but this is the real deal. A walled city only recently uncovered by archaeologist Yosef Garfinkel and his team, this hilltop has made headlines. In 2007 it was completely unknown. A year later it was the subject of stories in the *New York Times*, *National Geographic*, CNN, the BBC, and more. By 2018 a book about the excavations, *In The Footsteps of King David*, became a bestseller. Why? What archaeologists found here upended much of the accepted wisdom about King David's era.

As I've mentioned, many scholars, known as "biblical minimalists," had concluded the Israelites of David's time were still just a loose coalition of tribes, not yet organized into the wealthy, centrally organized empire described in the Bible as emerging under David. After all, they pointed out, there were no ruins of the sort of fortified cities you'd expect an empire to build. So clearly the Bible writers were either making up stories about King David or exaggerating his accomplishments.

Then this happened.

II
EXPLORING THE LOST CITY

Moments after we arrive, Danny is out of the car and bounding through the ruins, and as I race to catch up he shouts, "Look! Very rare!" He's pointing to the thick-walled remains of a massive gate. The construction is precise and of high quality, not crude at all, and impressive in scale. Just one of the stones, the one that forms the threshold, is estimated to weigh about eight tons.

As we wander the ruins even my amateur eyes can see this was not a primitive place. I walk between its thick double walls. The artifacts discovered here reveal a prosperous fortress engaged in international trade: thousands of pieces of pottery, swords and daggers, axes and arrowheads, game boards and Egyptian scarabs, luxury goods like alabaster jars and traces of wine and beer. Archaeologists also found "hammerstones," pieces of flint shaped by small hammers into streamlined balls, probably used as bullets for slings.

But how do the experts know this is an *Israelite* city? And how do they know for sure it's from *David's* era?

First, thousands of animal bones were found here. Sheep bones, cow bones, goat bones. Not one pig. That's significant because pork was forbidden to the Israelites.

Second, at Canaanite and Philistine sites there are lots of clay idols in the form of animals and humans, especially mother goddess figurines. Here? Not one. That's another marker of Israelite culture, since the Ten Commandments forbade graven images.

Third, part of an inscription was found here in an ancient form of Hebrew. It seems to be the first part of a Bible verse. *Thou shalt not…* Since that's a phrase repeated in the Mosaic law many times, it's likely these were Israelites.

Fourth, olive pits found here were taken to Oxford and carbon-dated by their scientists. They were found to be 3,000 years old (the olive pits, not the scientists). Exactly the time of David.

Fifth, there were baking trays. Hundreds of baking trays. I'm getting hungry just thinking about it.[1]

Significantly, there are no ruins of sophisticated, walled Israelite cities from before 1,000 AD. The lost city of Khirbet Qeiyafa suggests that rapidly, right around that time, the Israelites developed into an organized society capable of building large-scale cities like this. They were no longer just a bunch of poor, unskilled, weak tribes. The Bible's explanation? The leadership of David and his son Solomon.

I ask Danny how this discovery is impacting scholarship about David.

"For all the biblical minimalists trying to trash the Bible as a credible source for the time of David and Goliath, this site is a big problem," he says. "What was found here has definitely swung the pendulum back toward the traditional view, that the Bible can be seen as a valid historical source. It's not just religious text, it's also real history."

I really want to clarify this for the record, so I ask, "And you're saying that not as a religious leader with an axe to grind, but as a man of science, an archaeologist, an academic with a teaching position at a secular institution?"

"Yeah, totally," Danny affirms. "And wait till you see what's on the opposite side of the valley!" We climb back into his Jeep for another somewhat hair-raising trip down the hillside and across the narrow valley floor.

✦　　✦　　✦

When we get to the valley we suddenly skid to a halt and Danny announces, "But first we need to try my sling!" I try to keep up as he shoots out of the Jeep and lopes through the high grass to the dry creek bed that runs through the valley. He pulls a replica of an ancient sling out of his pocket and dares me to choose my own stone from the riverbed and try to launch it as David did. I'm a little nervous, because saying I'm uncoordinated is like saying Chewbacca is a little hairy. I've been known to stab myself in the cheek with my own fork if I don't pay careful attention while eating. My hand-eye coordination is so bad that I've wondered on occasion if my wrists have their own separate malevolent consciousness, like Doc Ock's arms in Spider-Man. But I find a nice-looking pebble, put it in the pocket of the sling, and spin it furiously—I tell myself, *You can do this! You've seen Thor twirl his hammer in all those Marvel movies!* (This is why I need to study the Bible more. A lot of my pep talks are grounded in Marvel movies.)

I envision Goliath in front of me. He's going for his sword. It's now or never. I let the stone fly.

And it whacks me right in the forehead. I see stars and hear Danny cracking up. When he finally catches his breath he says, "Well, I think I almost witnessed the world's first-ever suicide by slingshot."

Hey, what a fun diversion. As the egg on my head grows, I totter after Danny. We jump back into the SUV and zoom up another slope on the opposite side of the valley, dodging a tour bus and several scrambling civilians along the narrow road.

When we stop, we're facing the ruins of another ancient walled fortress. But this one, less than two miles away, is not Israelite. It's Philistine.

✿   ✿   ✿

Danny leaps up the hill and climbs the wall. "This would have been the headquarters of the Philistine army as it faced the Israelites 3,000 years ago," he explains, pointing across toward the hill we just explored.

This is how scientists now know where in the long Elah Valley these skirmishes between Israelite and Philistine forces likely took place: these twin cities mark the precise edges of the frontier. Then Danny stops, mid-sentence. "Hold on!" He jumps down and scoops up a handful of dirt. "Bring your water bottle!" He sprinkles water on his discovery to rinse away the dust and reveals a clay shard. "Yep, Philistine pottery," he concludes. He tosses it back on the ground. Just a broken piece with no unusual markings, so it's relatively uninteresting to an archaeologist like him, but to me it's one more bit of proof.

I linger at the edge of the hill, facing north, and picture the two armies facing each other in the valley right below me.

And another aspect of the story suddenly clicks. When I turn to my right I see the rocky hills that pile upward to Jerusalem and Bethlehem. When I look left, I see a patchwork of agricultural fields stretching toward the fertile coastal plain and the Mediterranean Sea beyond.

The ancient Israelites came from my right. Hill people.

The ancient Philistines came from my left. Sea People.

So this valley, which connects the hills to the coast, is the *inevitable* place for the Sea People and the Hill People to collide.

And that explains the standoff. The Philistines used armor and chariots—an advantage on flat ground, but once you get up in the hills, all that heavy iron is a disadvantage. The Israelites, on the other hand, didn't have much armor (except, the Bible says, for armor worn by Saul and his sons, which they probably stole from some Philistines). They did have snipers—expert archers and slingers. But on the flat plain, the agile but unarmored Israelites were no match for the stout swords and swift horses of the Philistines.

So it was a standoff. And standoffs are expensive. Something had to give.

That's why the solution proposed by a Philistine soldier gets attention. "Let's just have it out man-to-man," he shouts across the valley. "Your best fighter against me." Similar scenes are described in the battle traditions of many other ancient cultures. It's sometimes called "champion warfare," and typically took place when forces were at a stalemate. It wasn't ideal, but at least it was a way forward.

DIGGING DEEPER

23 AND ME AND THE PHILISTINES

In July 2019 a team of scientists working in Israel reported the results of their unusual ancestry project. They were able to retrieve DNA from 10 skeletons found in the ruins of the ancient Philistine city of Ashkelon, mentioned in the Bible. After analyzing this Philistine DNA and comparing it to genome material from other ancient human remains, they were able to determine conclusively for the first time that the Philistines originated from Europe, as some historians had theorized. This supports the hypothesis that they were part of the dreaded "Sea Peoples," invaders probably displaced from Europe during the Late Bronze Age Collapse.[2]

✳

III
FACING GIANTS

I rummage through the saddlebag slung over my shoulder looking for my battered travel Bible (and some aspirin for this splitting slingshot headache) and after I find it, I turn to 1 Samuel 17. Danny and I have spent all morning digging into the archaeology. Now I really want to dig into the story. Because I still need to answer a nagging question. *What's really the point?*

Right away I hit my first snag. The Bible says:

*"Then Goliath, a Philistine champion from Gath, came out
of the Philistine ranks to face the forces of Israel. He was
over nine feet tall!"*

1 SAMUEL 17:4 NLT

Hold on. A nine-foot giant? What's next, a magic beanstalk?
After hearing archaeolgoical conformation from Danny about
the general historical situation, this seems like a push right back
into Fantasyland.

Later I do a little research and find two ways to make sense
of this. First, is a nine-foot-plus height even possible? Well, the
tallest man in modern history was Robert Wadlow, who was
still growing when he died at age 24 at eight feet eleven inches,
so Goliath's height is probably not out of the range of human
genetic possibility.

But there's another option. I discover that the nine-foot-and-
change height is found only in the Masoretic text of the Hebrew
Bible (the ancient measurement is "six cubits and a span"). The
Masoretic text is named for a group of Jews, the Masoretes,
who meticulously hand-copied the Hebrew Bible into books
for scholars and synagogues to use from about 800 to 1000 AD.
While this became the authoritative text for rabbinic Judaism
and is consulted by all Christian Bible translators, the oldest copy
of the Masoretic text dates only from the ninth century after
Christ—in other words, about 1,900 years after David.

So how do we know that, over a period of 19 centuries,
manuscript copyists didn't, well, stretch Goliath's height? In
order to ensure that errors haven't crept into the Bible's text over
the centuries, modern Bible translators always consult the oldest
possible manuscripts and fragments. Where there are major
differences, Bibles indicate the alternate readings in footnotes

(and by the way, no variation yet found affects basic Christian or Jewish theology; variant readings tend to be these sorts of details about numbers and dates).

Intriguingly, in all the *older* manuscripts, like the 2,000-year-old Dead Sea Scrolls text of Samuel and the even earlier Greek translation called the Septuagint, Goliath's height is described as "four cubits and a span." Four. Not six. In American measurements, that's about six feet nine inches. So the *older* manuscripts—over a thousand years older than the Masoretic text—all agree on a *shorter* height for Goliath.[2] This would make Goliath about the height of an NBA athlete. For perspective, based on ancient skeletal remains, we know the average male height in David's era was about five and a half feet, three inches shorter than the average American male today.

If that older reading is the accurate one, then this wouldn't have been Jack facing the Jolly Green. It was more like Tom Cruise facing LeBron James. Not quite the picture I got in Sunday School, but in a fight I'd still put my money on LeBron.

Now couple Goliath's height with Philistine battle tech:

> *He had a bronze helmet on his head and wore a coat of*
> *scale armor of bronze weighing five thousand shekels.*
> *On his legs he wore bronze greaves (leg coverings) and a*
> *bronze javelin was slung on his back.*
>
> 1 SAMUEL 17:5,6 NIV

Quite a description. Basically the guy's armor-plated.

And for 40 days, every day and every night, this giant of a man comes out and demands everyone's attention. His shouts echo through the valley, "Choose a man to fight me! I defy the armies of Israel!" To add some emphasis, he even blasphemes the

Israelite God. If his shouts were texts, they would be punctuated with lots of those red-faced devil-head emojis. And what's the response? A stampede—in reverse. Every day, when the Israelites saw the man, they all ran from him in great fear (1 Samuel 17:24).

Note: They didn't fight. But they didn't go home either. They just did the same ineffective thing every single day. *For 40 days.*

In my experience, that's what fear always does. It leads to a paralysis of the will. You stare at the giant problem constantly, day after day, aware enough to stay worried, but too afraid to act.

Finally, somebody does something. A teenager, someone who was only at the battlefront because his dad sent him to bring (yes!) bread to his older brothers, accepts the challenge. He calmly collects five smooth stones from the brook (Why five? Probably because, as we learn later, the giant had brothers) and defeats Goliath with a sling, inspiring his army to victory.

So, again, what's the point?

It's easy to see how this tale became iconic for a people who always seemed to find themselves fighting for their land against larger, better-equipped foes—the Israelites were always the Davids standing against the Goliaths of surrounding nations.

But it has had lasting power not as some sort of Iron Age self-help talk; its appeal goes far deeper into the human psyche than that. Here's where a less-than-careful retelling of this story can sell it short. The way it's often taught sounds like *The Little Shepherd That Could*: David defeated a giant because he kept saying, "I think I can, I think I can." And though you may feel small, if you have faith in yourself, then you can do it too! Unicorn and confetti emojis!

Not quite the message of this story. Because in the really challenging times of life, faith in yourself is not enough. In fact, those are exactly the moments when faith in your own ability falters. That's what the rest of the Israelite army was experiencing. So what you need when you face the really big fears is faith in something bigger than your own strength, bigger than your skill, bigger than the biggest giant—faith in something that will never fail.

This is not a story about faith in yourself. This is a story about faith in *God*.

Great, but how do I stay focused on an unseen God when there's a very visible, distracting giant right in front of me (That's the problem with giants. They're so easy to see!)?

You know exactly what I mean. What's the huge fear yelling threats and curses in your valley right now, demanding all your attention every day and every night? For you it may be a giant practical need, a looming housing or financial or career struggle. It may be a titanic emotional problem, unforgiveness or bitterness or anxiety. Aging and death and disease are other Goliaths waiting to rumble into your valley. You may be facing gargantuan worries about your children or your bills or your marriage.

All giants have one thing in common. They are big and they are loud. They will paralyze you with fear if you let them capture your imagination.

My own species of giant, the anxiety I'm wrestling with on this trip, came into my life shortly after I began pastoring my current church. First I experienced alarming physical symptoms: insomnia, tunnel vision, chest pains, and shortness of breath. I ended up in the hospital because I thought I was having a heart attack or stroke. After a series of tests, the doctor concluded I was having textbook anxiety attacks.

Although I conquered that specific giant of anxiety attacks (more on that shortly), guess what I discovered? My Goliath had brothers. They rumble into my life at the most inopportune times, including this trip to Israel. Though I haven't had further anxiety attacks, anxiety-related pessimism and discouragement shout and challenge and distract me, and even blaspheme my God, and again I have to choose. Will I stare at these giants and listen to their threats, frozen in fear, or will I fight them?

IV
FIGHTING FEAR

As I read, I find four principles in David's story about fighting fear. I write them in my travel journal and, always trying to find mnemonic devices to help me remember things, organize them into the acronym **F-E-A-R**.

FIND OUT THE FACTS

This is the first thing David does:

> *David asked the men standing near him, "What will be done for the man who kills this Philistine and removes this disgrace from Israel?"*
>
> **1 SAMUEL 17: 26 NIV**

You know what I love about David here? Everyone else is focusing on the *risk*. He's focusing on the *reward*. Instead of obsessing on the problem, he immediately begins breaking it down, analyzing it, studying the benefits of beating it.

During my initial bout with anxiety attacks, I read every book I could find on handling anxieties. I learned an important truth: *good information breeds confidence.* Don't build mental monsters out of fear and worry.

Is your giant overcoming anxiety? Get the facts. There are so many great resources out there. Is it an illness? Get the facts. Educate yourself. Is it raising teens? Good luck. No, I mean, get facts. Ask advice. Read books.

ELIMINATE DEFEATIST THINKING

Defeatist thoughts are not just sad thoughts. Everyone gets those from time to time. That's just part of life; being sad is not bad. Defeatism goes further and says, "Don't even try. You will only fail." You need to cut off that kind of thinking.

Notice I didn't write, "eliminate negative *feelings*." Your feelings are largely out of your control. But you *can* control what you *think* about. This takes discipline. It may mean limiting your exposure to certain media or even certain friends. Because defeatism is contagious.

> Your feelings are largely out of your control. But you can control what you think about.

Look at the different ways David resists negative thinking. First, from his own relatives: Eliab, David's oldest brother...

...burned with anger at him and asked, "Why have you come down here? I know how conceited you are and how wicked your heart is; you came down only to watch the battle."

1 SAMUEL 17:28 NIV

Sometimes your worst criticism will come from your family. So what does David do? Very important phrase in verse 30: *"David then turned away to someone else…"*

Just… turn away. David didn't challenge his brother. He didn't try to win the argument. Remember, *rejection is not fatal.* It's just someone's opinion. You do not have to fight family while a giant is out there threating everyone. Choose your battles wisely.

> Rejection is not fatal. It's just someone's opinion.

Next, David had to resist defeatist thinking from an expert authority—King Saul, the greatest warrior in Israel:

> *"Don't be ridiculous!"* Saul replied. *"There's no way you can fight this Philistine and possibly win! You're only a boy, and he's been a man of war since his youth."*
>
> 1 SAMUEL 17:33 NLT

There will always be so-called experts who tell you why what *they're* afraid of doing can't be done by you. But David persisted:

> *"I have been taking care of my father's sheep and goats,"* he said. *"When a lion or a bear comes to steal a lamb from the flock, I go after it with a club and rescue the lamb from its mouth… I have done this to both lions and bears, and I'll do it to this pagan Philistine, too…"*
>
> 1 SAMUEL 17:34–36 NLT

Now what's funny to me is that I would've seen all this as a series of bad luck. *A lion attacked. And a bear attacked. And another lion and another bear. And now a giant! What am I, a magnet for trouble?* Not David.

> *"The LORD who delivered me from the paw of the lion and the paw of the bear will deliver me from the hand of this Philistine."*
>

David knows that the key to trusting God with your future is remembering how God has worked in your past. You can't see the future. That's what drives you crazy sometimes. But you *can* see the *past.* So think of the ways God answered prayer, gave you peace, performed a miracle in your life. Think especially of how God loved you so much that he sent his son Jesus to save you.

You and I also need to resist the temptation of negative thinking from *ourselves.* Are you your own worst critic and most vocal naysayer? I am. Sometimes I think it's my superpower. I am *Worst-Case-Scenario Man,* able to leap to grisly conclusions in a single bound. When my wife is five minutes late: *She's probably dead.* I get a pain in my knee: *Bone cancer, most likely.*

Maybe it stems from losing a father when I was not quite four (and consequently learning that sometimes the worst case scenario happens) but I really have to practice resisting my own defeatist thoughts. I need to learn not to constantly anticipate bad outcomes—because they usually don't happen, and I end up experiencing the *anxiety* of disaster when there's no *actual* disaster.

Saul then tells David, "Well, if you're going to try this, use my armor." Happens all the time. People want to tell you it can't be done. Then when it's clear you're going to try it anyway, they want to tell you how to do it.

David tries on Saul's armor, but it's too big for him and he refuses it. By the way, why is Saul's armor so big? According to 1 Samuel 9:2, Saul was head and shoulders taller than anyone else in Israel. So who should have been fighting the Philistine giant? Israel's giant! But Saul has forgotten the third key.

AFFIRM YOUR SOURCE OF STRENGTH

This is the key difference between mere positive *thinking* and positive *faith*. David didn't just use positive thinking. He didn't go running up to Goliath, "I think I can, I think I can!" He had positive faith. "I know I can because I know *God* can."

David calmly answers Goliath's insults with confident truth:

"You come against me with sword and spear and javelin, but I come against you in the name of the LORD Almighty... it is not by sword or spear that the LORD saves; for the battle is the LORD's..."

1 SAMUEL 17:45,47 NIV

The battle is the Lord's.

David's confidence is deeply rooted in one thing. He acts in the name of the Lord Almighty. He believes that he is a chosen member of God's chosen people, Israel, and that God has a plan for them.

In my observation, this is the very reason Christians often lack courage. They forget their *identity*, their *chosenness*, both individually and as part of God's people. As we saw in the last chapter, the Bible says if you are in Christ, God also chose *you*. You are part of His chosen *people*.

How can we better remember this?

One of the things that helped me so much during my anxiety attack phase, in addition to rest and exercise and medication, was this: I wrote Bible verses on several 3x5 cards, put a rubber band around them, put them in my back pocket like a wallet, and carried them with me everywhere I went. I even slept with them under my pillow. I read them three or more times a day, and often during the night, pulling them out whenever I heard the taunt of the giant.

These were some of the verses on those cards:

"So do not fear, for I am with you; do not be dismayed, for I am your God. I will strengthen you and help you; I will uphold you with my righteous right hand."

ISAIAH 41:10 NIV

"Do not be afraid, for I have ransomed you. I have called you by name; you are mine. When you go through deep waters, I will be with you. When you go through rivers of difficulty, you will not drown."

ISAIAH 43:1B–2A NLT

"I chose you. I appointed you to go and produce lasting fruit."

JOHN 15:16A NLT

But you are a chosen race, a royal priesthood, a holy nation, a people for his own possession, that you may proclaim the greatness of the One who called you out of darkness and into his marvelous light.

1 PETER 2:9 NIV

Notice how many times these promises are repeated: "I am with you;" "I have chosen you;" "I will strengthen you."

You may feel very small. But you are *strengthened* by someone bigger. Way bigger than any giant. The more you see yourself as part of a bigger plan, with strength from a bigger source, the less the giants will intimidate you.

✧　　✧　　✧

So now the tension is really mounting. David and Goliath have made their speeches. They approach each other on the battlefield.

And David does what no one has dared for 40 days.

> As the Philistine moved closer to attack him, David **ran quickly** toward the battle line to meet him.
>
> 1 SAMUEL 17:48 NIV

RUN TO BATTLE

After all is said and done, you have to stop just sitting there thinking about it, and start running to meet the challenge. You can get paralysis by analysis. At some point you just need to *act*. Like David did.

Someone once said, *action breeds courage*. Tennyson wrote, "I must lose myself in action, lest I wither in despair." I love that!

The more you see yourself as part of a bigger plan, with strength from a bigger source, the less the giants will intimidate you.

David lost himself in action while the rest of the army had been withering in despair for forty days.

As David sprints toward Goliath, the cacophony in the valley is stilled. Two armies hold their collective breath.

They hear Goliath's ponderous armor clanking. David's spinning sling whistling.

He lets it loose. The stone slices through the air.

Smack.

The End.

Forty days of stalling, 40 days of worrying, 40 days of anxiety, and the match lasts maybe two minutes. Goliath falls like a sack of rocks. David finishes him off with the giant's own sword. It's over. Days of delay—and a few moments of action solve the problem.

It can happen for you too.

Run to battle. Do something.

Action breeds courage.

Turn to action instead of despair. What happens if you just keep doing nothing? Your fear grows stronger. Your anxiety intensifies. You lose another hour of sleep. You delay any progress. What happens if you do something? You'll probably make some progress. You may just slay that giant.

Maybe you feel that all you have is a pebble's worth of ability versus a Goliath-sized problem. But so what? If God has chosen you, if God has a destiny for you, if God's Spirit is empowering you, who knows what you are setting into motion? Put your pebble into play—and see what happens next.

V

BARRIER BREAKER

The next sentence in this story is often overlooked, yet it's such an important detail:

> *Then the men of Israel and Judah surged forward with a shout and pursued the Philistines.*
>
> 1 SAMUEL 17:52 NIV

When did the people shout? When did they charge? Right after David had killed the giant.

I love to run, and a weird running fact that runners puzzle over is this: speed barriers that lasted for centuries seem to fall regularly once someone breaks that record. No one in recorded history had ever run a sub-four-minute mile until Roger Bannister did. Then in the next two years, 213 more people ran sub-four-minute miles! Bannister was the barrier-breaker for a generation of runners.

And David was the barrier-breaker for the Israelites. Once he killed the giant, the rest of the army surged forward.

As John Maxwell points out, that's what can happen every time you face a giant in your life. The minute you knock it down, other people will say, "We can do that too!" Think of how you might inspire people around you, your own children, your friends, when you can tell them honestly and transparently about the lion or bear or giant that God helped *you* defeat! This is what helps lead people into faith, into sobriety, into achievement. Be open about your struggles and honest about your progress. Your testimony can be a barrier-breaker for others.

ACT ON IT

The bottom line is this: *act on what you say you believe.*

As I read my Bible on the Elah Valley hillside, something strikes me. Every single person in that Israelite army knew about God's deliverance of their ancestors—all those great stories, from the famine to Pharaoh, from Jericho to Judges. They knew how Abraham had been chosen, how Moses had been chosen, how the Israelites had been chosen. They knew God's promise to Joshua centuries before:

> *"Be strong and courageous! Do not be afraid or discouraged. For the LORD your God is with you wherever you go."*
>
> JOSHUA 1:9 NLT

In other words, they knew—and my guess is, they would have said they believed—*the same exact stuff David believed.* Theologically they were there. But they did not *act* on what they said they *believed.*

Let me be blunt. You say you believe God will help you, you say you believe He is sovereign and works all things together for good, you say he loves you, but the proof of belief is in the action. If you believe that, then stop worrying. If you believe that you are part of something bigger, then devote yourself to that higher cause with confidence. Act. Contribute. Serve.

Do what you can... as part of God's plan... and remember: the battle is the Lord's.

✦ ✦ ✦

My reverie on the hill overlooking the beautiful Elah Valley is interrupted suddenly by fat raindrops plopping onto the pages of my journal. I look up and see dark clouds and run for cover.

That reminds me: *the rain will fall.*

Even if you live with the confident faith of David and see wonderful victories, that doesn't mean you'll see an unending string of good fortune. Some Christians assume that, if they only have the right kind of confident faith, they will kill every giant and never experience defeat. Not true.

Sometimes you'll endure a long parade of failure before the next victory. As David is about to discover. When his path to the throne leads him underground. ✦

DIGGING DEEPER

MAGNUM FORCE

Scholars of ancient warfare have demonstrated that ancient slings were not mere kids' toys.

These were not *slingshots*. These were *slings*, two long strips of leather that held a small leather pouch between them. Slingers would place a stone—often a rock expertly shaped by a craftsman into an oblong bullet-like form—into the pouch. Then, grasping the ends of the leather straps, they would spin, aim, and let loose. As the rock shot forward, it would also be spinning rapidly.

Analysis by German researcher Joerg Sprave showed that, within their range, ancient slings had about the same stopping power as a modern .44 Magnum (Although he specifically analyzed Roman slings, the technology was very similar to slings used by Israelites.).[4]

What about accuracy? *National Geographic* reported the results of another experiment. At a firing range, skilled users of ancient-style slings were pitted against handgun experts. The slings were *more* accurate than a modern handgun at a range up to 30 meters. Other tests revealed that a trained slinger could hit a target smaller than a human being from 130 yards away.[5] Essentially, Goliath brought a spear to a gunfight.

✳

THREE

FINDING LIGHT IN THE DARKNESS

I

AN ANCIENT CAVE, SOMEWHERE IN JUDEA

To stay on David's trail, I have to chase him underground.

One unique feature of Israel's geography: it's the land of a thousand caves. When you know what to look for, you see them everywhere, dotting nearly every hillside and ravine. Turns out the limestone in the hills here is perfect for cave formation. It's probably one reason the earliest hominid fossils outside Africa have been found in Israel—the numerous natural caves were ready-made homes.

Then ancient people sped up the natural process of cave-making, digging into the soft and easily hewn stone, riddling the earth with miles of man-made tunnels. For millennia people have used these caves as homes and hideouts, storerooms and stables, water cisterns and worship spaces, granaries and gravesites. The caves of Israel have hidden secret treasure and sacred manuscripts. And at least one future king.

"You could live underground in Israel for years and never be found," Danny tells me. Which is probably just what David intends in the story we'll explore next. During a time of deep emotional darkness, David finds himself in a physical landscape that mirrors his soul's distress.

It was David's cave time.

No one knows just how many caves there are in Israel.

"It's nearly impossible to count them, because new ones are discovered every day," said Professor Amos Frumkin, director of the Cave Research Unit at the Hebrew University of Jerusalem's geography department, in an interview with Israel's channel 21. "Right now we have about 1,200 registered caves in our database, but I can estimate roughly that there are many thousands more."[1]

In one national park alone, Beit Guvrin-Maresha, there are 480 known caves, including the Bell Cave with 70 connected bell-shaped caverns, the Maze Cave consisting of about 30 interconnected chambers, and the Bathtub Cave with ancient restrooms. In the territory David traveled most frequently, from the Elah Valley down to Beersheva, there are thousands of caves, most unregistered on any database or map. Some are massive. In one, a labyrinth of subterranean passageways stretches for over six miles.

If you want to hide, there is probably not a better spot on earth than Israel.

✧   ✧   ✧

To personally experience an Israelite cave, I'm travelling back into the West Bank today. My local guide, a moonlighting dental hygienist named Johnny, says he knows a cave most tourists never see. It's perched on the edge of a small valley near Bethlehem.

Johnny takes us through a neighborhood, past a church, and down an alley until we emerge in an open field where, peering over crumbling stone walls, we see a valley below. Johnny waves us forward. "The cave is just down here!" We clamber down the sloping cliffs and then through a ruined house until we find the entrance. As caverns go, this one seems pretty harmless, just a semi-circular opening in the hillside. Johnny says in ancient times it was used as a kind of natural barn. Okay, kind of cool, but in a few minutes I'm ready to go, a little disappointed, if I'm honest.

Then as we're about to climb out, Johnny stops, turns, lowers his voice an octave, and slowly says the fateful words, "Of course... you may want to explore... further..."

Say what? He walks back to a place in the cave where faint light seems to cast a deep shadow. And puts his hand right through the wall.

At least, that's what it looks like. What seemed a shadow is really a wrinkle in the rock, a natural fissure leading to a tunnel that worms its way through the mountain. "There's another exit up the hill," Johnny says, pointing into the darkness. "You have to crawl through the tunnel to get to it, though. Not for everyone."

Let me stop the story to observe that there are two kinds of people: the kind who can't resist a cave and the kind who wouldn't go into a dark hole in the ground if a pack of wolves were chasing them. I guess I'm the first kind. "I'm up for it! Let's go!"

"Uhhhh... Tell you what. You go ahead." Johnny demurs. "I'll walk up the hill with Laurie and meet you at the other side."

Should have probably taken that as a warning but instead I announce (with a hint of superiority) that I'll explore the cave and meet the surface-dwellers at the other exit, "like Indiana Jones!" What's more, I loudly vow that I will not use my modern tech to light the path. I want to experience this cave as the ancients did. In the dark.

So I plunge in.

Maybe it's because my eyes are now useless in the absolute dark of the cave, but every other sense seems suddenly amplified. I smell the damp. Taste the mineral air. Hear the invisible stones skittering around my feet as I kick them forward. At least I hope those are stones.

I reach out to try and touch the wall ahead, to find the end of the darkness. But it seems to stretch forever into nothingness, my hand grasping, my fingers flailing, the void yawning.

So each step is a little shorter as I grow increasingly concerned I'll discover a surprise tunnel twist with my forehead or walk right off a ledge. Soon I'm shuffling more than walking, one little half-step at a time, bent over, like an old man in the dark, the cave quickly quenching pride and progress. I feel a vague anxiety rising. *How much longer does this go on anyway?*

I shake my head at how ridiculous my feelings are, try to swallow them. But my primal reaction against darkness (*"An ancient darkness,"* my imagination now narrates in its best movie-trailer voice, *"a darkness that from ages past has never seen a sunrise..."*) is proving hard to suppress.

I am rapidly changing into the second kind of person. The panicked thoughts start stampeding. Maybe I should turn back, maybe I took a wrong turn somewhere, maybe I am headed into the belly of the mountain where I'll never be found... and how well do I know Johnny anyway?

Finally I cheat, take out my iPhone, and flick on its flashlight app to shed some light on the situation. All it helps me see is more cave, cave before me, cave behind me, cave beneath me, cave above me, cave on my left, cave on my right, cave without end amen, the tunnel twisting and turning into the darkness ahead. I want to go back. I want to get out. I want to sit down and cry like a baby. The one direction I don't want to go? Forward. Into the darkness. I keep reminding myself, This is not a dead end cave. *This is a tunnel. This is a tunnel. This is a tunnel.*

I know it sounds absurd, because it actually only takes a few minutes to get through, but I can't explain the relief I feel when I see the glimmer of light ahead. I surge forward (making sure I put my iPhone in my pocket so no one figures out how freaked I was) and emerge in a deep pit somewhere on the hill. Above me I see sunshine and hear my wife's voice. I climb out to greet her, faking swagger: "Yep, pretty cool cave."

"Scary?" my wife asks.

"Nah."

"Mmmm-hmmm. Better turn off your iPhone flashlight, Dr. Jones."

I glance down and see the phone light shining through my pocket. Dang. Busted.

Would I do it again? Of course. Because now I know exactly how long the cave is. Because now I could go through it with an easy hope born of experience. And because now Johnny tells me he took some fifth-graders through it last week.

But my guess is, the first time in any cave seems at least a little surreal and suffused with a primitive fear. And the inevitable questions: How long does this go on? Can I trust my guide? Is there anyone else in here with me?

Those are questions David must have had in his own cave, as his life quickly turns from dream-come-true to nightmare-without-end.

II
LEAVING IT ALL BEHIND

When we last left David, he "was prospering in all his ways, for the LORD was with him." (1 Samuel 18:14) He defeats Goliath, becomes a celebrity, people even compose a popular song about him, he marries King Saul's daughter, gets exempted from all taxes, he's suddenly rich. It's all good. Then suddenly it's all bad.

When Saul saw how successful he was, he was afraid of him.
1 SAMUEL 18:15 NIV

Saul's jealous. So jealous he urges his son Jonathan and all his aides to assassinate David. Saul even tries to kill David himself. Twice.

So David starts running. There's a phrase, "David fled and escaped," that appears over and over again in the next few chapters as David narrowly dodges Saul's attacks:

> *David fled and escaped...* 1 SAMUEL 19:10 ESV
>
> *David fled away and escaped...* 1 SAMUEL 19:12 ESV
>
> *David fled and escaped...* 1 SAMUEL 19:18 ESV
>
> *David fled...* 1 SAMUEL 20:1 ESV
>
> *David rose and fled that day...* 1 SAMUEL 21:10 ESV
>
> *So David... escaped.* 1 SAMUEL 22:1 ESV

And every time he has to take off, he leaves something behind. Look at six essential parts of David's support system that he lost:

- *Position* (1 Samuel 19:10) He loses his place in the king's court, his job in times of peace.

- *Prosperity* (1 Samuel 18:11) In one night David has to leave his home. All his fortune. All his weaponry. All his baking trays.

- *Partner* (1 Samuel 19:12) His wife, Saul's daughter Michal, tells him to leave her and run for his life.

- *Prophet* (1 Samuel 19:18; 20:1) Samuel, probably an old man by now, has been David's mentor and advisor. But the frenetic pace of David's escapes proves to be too much for him. He stays behind in a place called Naioth while David moves on.

- *Peer* (1 Samuel 20:42) At the end of chapter 20, David bids a hasty goodbye to his best friend Jonathan, King Saul's son. They will never see each other alive again.

- *Pride* (1 Samuel 21:10–15) To save his own life, David does the unthinkable: He goes to Gath, the city of Goliath, believing Saul will never follow him there. But some officers in the Philistine army recognize him. In order to keep them from killing him, David pretends he is insane. The Bible says he scratches crazy marks on doors and lets saliva run down his beard. The Philistine king makes this interesting comment to his men: "Must you bring me a madman? We already have enough of them around here!"

Then it gets worse.

III
CAVE TIME

So David left Gath and escaped to the cave of Adullam.

1 SAMUEL 22:1 ESV

Today, Adullam Caves is a national park in Israel. The cave traditionally associated with David is massive. When you first crawl inside, it seems about the size of a large room in an average house. But keep walking, around the corner, and you'll find yourself in a series of tunnels that connect various vast natural caverns. You could literally hide an army in here.

David will need that space:

And everyone who was in distress, and everyone who was in debt, and everyone who was bitter in soul, gathered to him... about four hundred men.

1 SAMUEL 22:2 ESV

In his classic work on David, Charles Swindoll analyzes the three Hebrew words used in this verse to describe these men:[2]

Zuk means not only "in distress," but "under pressure, under stress." So here come hundreds of people on the brink of a breakdown.

Nashah means "to have a number of creditors." These are not just guys who can't pay their bills, who have no resources; they also have bill collectors angrily seeking them. David's trying to escape detection and they're making it a lot harder.

Maar nephesh means "to be in bitterness of soul, to have been wronged and mistreated." Welcome to a bunch of malcontents convinced the world has it in for them.

So not only does David lose all his good stuff, he gains a bunch of high-maintenance hangers-on. In the comedy "What About Bob?" Bill Murray plays a patient who follows his psychiatrist everywhere, constantly insisting, "I need, I need!" I picture David with 400 Bobs.

Put all this together, and you can see how his life has hit an all-time low.

✦   ✦   ✦

You may be there now. Right next to David. Living in a cave.

Yours may be the cave of cancer, the darkness of disease. You may find yourself deep in the ditch of dreary work or age or unemployment or financial struggles. You may be in the haunted hollow of a broken heart, rebellious children, a lost love. Or you're in the cave without clear cause, the strange darkness of despair. You find yourself oppressed, fearing what's around the corner, yet you don't even know how you got there—or how to get out.

I get it. As I mentioned, when I started this book I found myself tumbling into a cave of my own, a ditch of deep discouragement. I could not shake the feeling that my work as a pastor was all meaningless, that my life had no impact, that I might as well quit writing in the middle of this book. To you it may not make sense, but then deep discouragement rarely does.

I do wonder now if God let me descend into that cave to help me remember what soul-darkness feels like. It's like He was saying, "So you want to avoid clichés and trite advice in this book? Then you need to feel what people in caves feel."

Well, it feels terrible. It feels just like that cave in Israel. Even now I struggle to find words to describe the sensation— deep desolation, pitch-black limbo, spinning slowly down an endless dark mine shaft. Lost.

Maybe that's one reason we need poets and artists like David, not to offer solutions but to help us find words to express our feelings. And to be buoyed by the recognition that someone gets it. When I find that someone else knows what my cave feels like, even if they offer no solutions, the discovery of that shared experience fosters hope. Because it means someone else has been there before—and *survived to write about it.*

When I discovered this poem from Michael Quiost's book, "Prayers," it lifted my spirit just to know someone else had been in the cave before me.

Lord, it is dark.
Lord, are you here in my darkness?
Your light has gone out.

Everything seems grey and somber as
when a fog blots out the sun.

Everything is an effort, everything is difficult,
    and I am heavy-footed and slow.
Every morning I am overwhelmed at
    the thought of another day.

I long for an end.

I go through the same motions each day,
    but I know they are meaningless.
I walk, but I know I am getting nowhere.
I speak, and my words seem empty.
Ideas themselves escape me, and I find it hard to think.

It wouldn't matter, except that I am alone.
I am alone.

You have taken me far, Lord. I followed you,
    and now, in the middle of the desert, at
    night, suddenly you have disappeared.

Lord, it is dark.
Lord, are you here in my darkness?
Do you love me still?
Or have I wearied you?

Lord, answer!

Answer.

It is dark.[3]

These are the very emotions expressed by David as he sits in the darkness of his cave.

IV
SURVIVING SOUL DARKNESS

We know precisely how David felt when he went through all this. He wrote two psalms while living in the cave—Psalm 57 and Psalm 142. These psalms don't explain how to *eliminate* cave times from your life. Cave times will hit you, one way or another. These psalms help you realize that you are not alone, that other people—other great, famous people—have felt exactly the same way. If you have anxiety or feel discouraged, you are not weird, a spiritual failure, or hopeless.

These "cave psalms" also demonstrate some strategies for surviving the cave times of life. Obviously, and I can't stress this enough, don't go it alone. Seek help from a strong friend, a pastor, a professional counselor. Yet David also models four constructive steps that you can initiate yourself, steps that keep you moving through the darkness. I've been living this, and I can tell you honestly that these have really helped me.

1. RELEASE YOUR CONCERNS TO GOD

In these "cave psalms" David doesn't hold back his frustrations in any way.

> *I cry out to the LORD;*
> *I plead for the LORD's mercy.*
> *I pour out my complaints before him*

and tell him all my troubles.
When I am overwhelmed,
 you alone know the way I should turn.
Wherever I go,
 my enemies have set traps for me.
I look for someone to come and help me,
 but no one gives me a passing thought!
No one will help me;
 no one cares a bit what happens to me.

PSALM 142:1–4 NLT

Look at those verbs: "cry out," "plead," "pour out," "tell." When you're confused or angry or frustrated, let it rip in your prayers. Say what you feel. This example from the Bible has been so helpful to me. And right now, it's almost counter-cultural.

Psychologist Steven Hayes says our whole culture has fallen victim to "feel-goodism," the false idea that bad feelings ought to be eliminated or denied.[4] This intolerance toward emotional pain puts us at odds with a basic truth about real life: sometimes we just feel bad. That is not wrong or sinful. It's just human. So trying to deny or bury every feeling of frustration and sadness leads, ironically, to even more frustration and sadness—as we get frustrated that we haven't been able to conquer our sadness!

Rather than denying it or burying it, talk to God about it. He can take it.

In the cave times, really your only options are *confession* or *repression*. When you honestly *confess* how you feel to God, you are dealing with reality. When you deal with reality, you can find healing. When you *repress*, you are on the road to denial, which is at the root of so much that's negative and unproductive.

That's why David never says, "Everything's fine! I am feeling victorious! It's all a blessing! I am an unquenchable optimist!" He basically says, "Hey, God? Everything stinks right now." So many Christians believe they must try to pretend the bad things are not happening, that everything's okay... but you won't find that example in the Bible.

Quick dad joke digression. It reminds me of the story about three guys who end up in hell: a seminary student, a fundamentalist, and a positive thinker. The student says, "My Bible teachers were very precise; if I had only listened to them, I wouldn't be here." The fundamentalist says, "My pastor preached all those hellfire and brimstone sermons; if I had responded, I wouldn't be here." And the positive thinker sits in the corner, rocking back and forth, repeating over and over, "It's not hot and I'm not here. It's not hot and I'm not here."

A lot of people go through tough times they could actually learn and grow from—but they never do. Why not? Because they're in denial. *"It's not hot and I'm not here."*

Pretending there's never any tragedy in your life is going to take a lot of pretending. Don't repress, confess.

2. REALIZE WHERE YOU ARE POWERLESS

Ever feel like you can't handle life? Guess what? Sometimes you can't! And admitting that is a key to receiving support from others and from God. Look at this surprising admission from David:

> *Hear my cry,*
> *for I am very low.*
> *Rescue me from my persecutors,*
> *for they are too strong for me.*

PSALM 142:6 NLT

That's a very honest phrase: *"They are too strong for me!"* David's in a spot that even he, the great giant killer, cannot handle. The situation was out of his control. David could not change Saul's mind. David couldn't change the army's orders. He couldn't prevent others from betraying his location to Saul's men. The wise thing he does here is, he admits it.

The most common mistake I make when things are truly out of my control? *I try to control them.* But I can't control other people, I can't control their opinions of me, I can't control the past, I can't control the future, I can't control most things.

Sometimes, and it takes wisdom to see this, you need to stop trying to control things you can't control anyway and crawl into the arms of God until the crisis is over. And that's the next point.

> Intolerance toward emotional pain puts us at odds with a basic truth about being human: Sometimes we just feel bad. That's not wrong or sinful.

3. RELAX IN GOD'S LOVING ARMS

Look at these verses from the cave:

> *Then I pray to you, O LORD.*
> *I say, "You are my place of refuge.*
> *You are all I really want in life."*
>
> **PSALM 142:5 NLT**

Have mercy on me, O God, have mercy on me,
    for in you my soul takes refuge.
I will take refuge in the shadow of your wings
    until the disaster has passed.

PSALM 57:1 NIV

Refuge. That's one of David's favorite words for God, used over forty times in the book of Psalms. What a great word to describe God! When people are making our lives miserable, we often want God to be a warrior, or a judge, or an avenger. But God does not always play those roles (although he promises he will eventually). However, he is *always* in the role we need most: a refuge. A place to go to hide "until the disaster has passed."

> Even in the darkness of your cave, he is still whispering to you, "Beloved."

David was learning an important lesson. Stripped of everything, he learned God still loved him. He was still, as his name affirmed, "beloved" by God.

And God still loves you. Even if everything seems to be taken away from you. Even in the darkness of your cave, he is still whispering to you, *"Beloved."*

Sometimes the enemy chasing you into the cave isn't another person; it's your own emotional state. But how do you fight a vague feeling of heaviness? In my own struggle with this I've tried to analyze the precise reasons I sometimes see the world through grey lenses—and I don't always get very far. I really don't know exactly why I am feeling the way I am. My guess is, you can relate. There have been times you've been completely perplexed by your emotions, unable to understand yourself.

The good news is, your Creator completely understands you, even when you don't! In another psalm, David writes,

> O LORD, *you have examined my heart*
>   *and know everything about me.*
> *You know when I sit down or stand up.*
>   *You know my thoughts even when I'm far away.*
>
> PSALM 139:1,2 NLT

When your own emotions shove you into the cave zone, you can still relax in the loving arms of the one who totally gets you. He sees, he understands, and he still calls you *beloved*.

4. REMEMBER GOD HAS A PURPOSE FOR YOU

David is told he'll be king—but that doesn't happen for years. Instead, he has many failures and false starts. You may feel your life has followed a similar trajectory. So much early promise. Now you feel like you're in life's waiting room. Be encouraged. Don't give up! God still has a destiny for you.

It's tough to wait. I get it. I don't like delays. I don't even like going to meetings. I like to get stuff done, check things off my to-do list. I feel best if, at the end of a day, I can look back and call it "productive." The most frustrating thing for

> Stop trying to control things you can't control and crawl into the arms of God until the crisis is over.

me is to feel my time is being wasted, that results are taking forever to manifest.

I have a hunch David felt the same way. He was the classic man of action, yet now he feels his life is on hold. But watch what he writes:

> *I cry out to God Most High,*
>> *to God who will fulfill his purpose for me.*
>>>> **PSALM 57:2 NLT**

God *who will fulfill his purpose for me*. When David was anointed by Samuel, he was told God had a purpose for him. So David chooses to believe that promise now: though things may look desperate, he still has a destiny. Though he is currently powerless to change his situation, the all-powerful God will still fulfill his purpose for him.

YOU HAVE A DESTINY

This sense of *destiny*, of forward motion into a new and promised future, is a characteristic of the Bible entirely lacking from the ancient literature of the surrounding cultures. They emphasized not destiny, but fate. *No matter what you try in life, your fate is sealed. The gods have it in for you. They will never let you get ahead.*

That's why many Greek plays are tragedies, ending in gloom and resignation. Ultimately, they assert, tragedy awaits all humans. There's no real progress, no straight timeline leading somewhere good. Everything resets after you, back to zero again, a never-ending circle. That's the *fate* mindset. It's making a comeback in our culture as fewer people have a biblical viewpoint, and just see their lives as a few short meaningless years bracketed by infinite non-existence. There's no purpose. Only guaranteed doom.

But the Bible teaches the *destiny* mindset, that there is a way forward, that God is ultimately in control and is working all things together for an ultimate good according to His plan. There is a meta-narrative, a grand story God is writing that will knit together all of our individual stories into something beautiful. There will be justice, healing, and resolution.

That means He has a destiny for *you* to fulfill as part of that plan, and if you yield your life to His control you *will* live to fulfill that destiny. Your life's efforts will not be in vain.

> Your down times are not evidence your life ends in *tragedy*; they are part of the story God will knit together into a *destiny*.

Your down times are not evidence your life ends in *tragedy*; they are part of the story God will knit together into a *destiny*.

DESTINY MINDSET OR FATE MINDSET?

As I muse on David's story it strikes me that in my discouraged state leading up to this trip I'd been slipping from the *destiny* mindset into the *fate* mindset. Emotionally, I hadn't been anticipating victory. I'd been expecting tragedy. Every day, I woke up and wondered what else would go wrong.

I think this is at the core of anxiety and discouragement for all of us: the idea that the other shoe is going to drop any minute now, that tragedy is around the corner, that all my efforts are futile, I'm not making a difference, life has no ultimate purpose.

To get out of this muddy, moody hole I'm in, I need to keep my new habit of reminding myself daily: *I don't have a fate, I have a destiny*. It is secured not by my abilities, but by God's anointing, God's choosing, God's will. He will sovereignly use even the failures, even the dark times of my life, to achieve his great plan.

NOT ABOUT ME

This is helpful because it's the opposite of self-absorbed thinking. One very bad habit I can get into when I feel despair is constantly thinking about myself, my feelings, my difficulties. I call it "ingrown eyeballs."

Most attempts at solving that kind of self-centered despair usually amount to replacing your negative thoughts with positive thoughts. That's okay in the short term, but that strategy has a weakness: it's still all about me. I'm still making myself the center of my thought life. That makes it easy to slip from positive thoughts right back to negative—because I'm still in the habit of thinking about myself.

> I don't have a fate, I have a destiny.

To paraphrase C.S. Lewis, the solution is not to think *more* of myself, and the solution is not to think *less* of myself; the solution is to think *of myself less*. Think of God more. Get lost in wonder.

This is exactly what David does in his cave. He is honest about his trouble, but turns his attention to God.

> *I am surrounded by fierce lions*
> *who greedily devour human prey—*
> *whose teeth pierce like spears and arrows,*
> *and whose tongues cut like swords.*
> *Be exalted, O God, above the highest heavens!*
> *May your glory shine over all the earth.*
>
> PSALM 57:4,5 NLT

David was still in the cave. But he started to see a glimmer of glory.

His cave psalms never offer trite advice along the lines of "Tomorrow will be a better day" or "This isn't really so bad after all." Without denying his painful situation, David shifts his focus from the pain to something much more profound, to the God who writes the meta-narrative that arches far above our personal narratives, the story that encompasses all our stories—and will ultimately work them all together for good. That's how to get spiritual night-vision.

✻   ✻   ✻

Vaclev Havel was imprisoned in 1977 in his home country of Czechoslovakia for peacefully opposing the oppressive communist government. Like David, Havel was known both as a political leader and an artist. Then everything was taken from him by rulers who felt threatened by his popularity. It was his cave time.

At first he was consumed by frustration at his situation. He grew very sick and almost died. One day, he gazed in weakness over the prison wall and saw the very top of a tree. As he wrote his wife, Olga, suddenly he was...

> *...overcome by a sensation that is difficult to describe: all at once I seemed to rise above all the coordinates of my momentary existence in the world into a kind of state outside of time in which all the beautiful things I had ever seen and experienced existed at once...I felt a sense of reconciliation, indeed of almost gentle assent to the...course of events, and this combined with a carefree determination to face what had to be faced. A profound amazement*

at the sovereignty of Being became a dizzying sensation
of tumbling endlessly into the abyss of its mystery; an
unbounded joy at being alive, at having been given the
chance to live through all that I have lived through, and at
the fact that everything has a deep and obvious meaning.
I was flooded with a sense of ultimate happiness and
harmony... I would even say that I was 'struck by love'...[6]

He was later released from prison and became the leader of his nation.

Want the power to see in the dark? That's where it comes from. Don't gaze endlessly into your own misery. Lose yourself in God's mystery.

> Don't gaze endlessly into your own misery. Lose yourself in God's mystery.

For Havel, all it took to spark wonder was the top of a tree. Can you find a tree, a forest, a field? Try staring for a while. At least you won't be staring only at your sorrows. And you may just see a glimmer of light.

Remember: The One who lovingly created all you see also created and loves you. And still has a plan for you.

There's something else David does in the cave that gives him some glow-in-the-dark hope. It's so obvious it's easy to miss. *Music.* These psalms were songs.

Music has an amazing ability. Long after my mother's Alzheimer's disease rendered her incapable of conversation, she was still able to sing the lyrics of many beautiful old hymns of the faith. I would start a song like "Great Is Thy Faithfulness" and she would instantly perk up. I watched her body language change as confusion rolled away and peace took over. I learned that music can impact our souls at a deep level long after most of our cognitive capabilities are gone.

I find music to be key in my cave times too. It distracts me from my morbid thoughts, lifts my spirit, reminds me of truth in a way that's poetic and not preachy.

Yet it's strange that, though I know this to be true, when I'm really in the depths, I tend to forget about music. I have to keep reminding myself to refocus through song. As did David. Toward the end of one of his cave songs David reminds himself,

> ...I can sing your praises!
> Wake up, my heart!
> Wake up, O lyre and harp!
> I will wake the dawn with my song.
> I will thank you, Lord, among all the people.
> I will sing your praises among the nations.
>
> PSALM 57:7B–10 NLT

It's like he's remembering, "Oh yeah, I have that resource! I am not just going to sit and stew all night long. I am going to find comfort in song until morning."

These days you don't need to be a skilled musician like David; everyone can access great music 24/7 in a variety of ways. And this doesn't mean just "happy" songs. Many of David's psalms are not exactly "positive, encouraging music." Haunting, hard songs can be helpful when they're directed to God. Because they keep you in the *relationship* with God, and it's in that relationship that you find strength.

V
IT'S NOT A CAVE, IT'S A TUNNEL

Back in that cave near Bethlehem, I made an uncomfortable discovery. When you're in a completely dark cave and feel panic building in your chest, you have two overwhelming desires—to go back the way you came, or to sit down and cry.

The one thing you simply do not want to do, the one thing I had to force myself to do? *Move forward*. But that's the way out.

You may feel like you're in a cave. And you keep looking back at the good old days, back at the entrance. Or you sit in the darkness of loss or disaster.

> Just because you're chosen and blessed and destined does not mean you're immediately mature and perfect and spiritually successful.

But I want to tell you something. It's not a cave. It's a *tunnel*. The Bible promises, it's a tunnel. So *keep moving forward*, no matter how many twists and turns there are, no matter how dark it gets. Wake up each morning and take one step at a time into your future.

There's a light ahead. Maybe just a glimmer now. But it's there. David always comes back, even in his most pessimistic cave songs, to perceive that light, to say something along these lines: "I do not understand this at all. But I know this. God reigns."

Do you believe that? That God still reigns? That God will work out his purpose for you no matter what you are going through? That you are chosen and you still have a great future, here and in heaven? That there's an end to the darkness?

If you are on the floor of the cave and finding that hard to believe, then let me believe it for you. I believe God can use anything, even whatever's happening in your life right now, to accomplish something you could never have imagined. I *know* this to be true. I have seen it happen again and again, in my life and in the lives of others.

I really want you to hear this, particularly if you are a relatively new believer. There's so much pressure on young Christians to be early bloomers spiritually, to be totally dialed right away, to never have struggles. But just because you're chosen and blessed and destined does not mean you're immediately mature and perfect and spiritually successful. There may be years spent on the run and in caves. You will fail. You may relapse. It doesn't mean that what you've been told about God or about yourself is false. It just means life is life. There's darkness and confusion and pain and failure before the coronation, even in the lives of these Bible heroes.

> God still calls you *beloved. He will fulfill his destiny for you.*

But as with David, God's purpose for you has not changed. God still calls you *beloved. He will fulfill his destiny for you.*

In fact, he will use even this cave time for good.

Think of David. Anointed as a young man by Samuel to be the next king, he probably wonders how that's ever going to happen. When he's selected as Saul's favorite musician, he likely thinks, *This is my big break.* Then he's besties with the king's son Jonathan. More court connections. Better yet, he becomes a celebrity by defeating Goliath. Destiny assured. He's the golden boy! Then what happens? The bottom drops out.

But do you get it? What truly forged David into a king was actually not any of the seemingly promising events that happened before his cave time. It's in the stink and squalor and sadness of the cave that David starts his true trajectory to the throne. In exile he is forged into the leader he is meant to be. And it's in our caves that you and I are made into the people God wants us to be.

> It's in the stink and squalor and sadness of the cave that David starts his true trajectory to the throne.

Remember all those poor, destitute, indebted, homeless men who crowded into the cave with David? The Bible says he became their captain, and they were the core of his first little band of followers. All these rejects, led by David the reject, became an army of rejects that eventually—after many years—turned into the loyal palace guard once David became king. These weak and worried wanderers became memorialized as "mighty men."

Redeeming cave times. That's what God does.

Think of the icon of Christianity. *The cross.* It was the Roman Empire's way of saying, "Dead End. Dream Over." So why do millions of people now wear crosses around their necks? Even if they don't have a sophisticated theological understanding, at a soul-deep level they know this symbol stands for God working through the worst thing to bring about the best thing.

Jesus was dead on that cross. Finished. Then he went into the darkest kind of cave. The tomb. Alone.

But it wasn't over. In an act that changes all our cave times, God raised Jesus from that that tomb. His death and resurrection brought us life.

God specializes in using dead ends and dark caves for his purposes.

Now, that truth didn't make King Saul's murderous actions right. It didn't erase all of David's pain. It may not have shortened his cave time by even a day. But David's belief in this truth did one thing. It gave David hope. Hope that there was a light ahead.

✦   ✦   ✦

If you're in a cave right now, you probably feel like you're all alone. I get it. It's dark. It's hard to see anyone else. But the truth is, there are lots of us in there with you. Like me. And many of your other brothers and sisters. And in that cave, in the dark, you are actually walking step by step right on same trail with David— and with the Lord who loves you both so much. ✦

DIGGING DEEPER

DAVID THE MUSICIAN

David is identified as the author of 73 *psalms*, ancient songs written for worship. Their lyrics are preserved in the biblical Book of Psalms. It contains 150 psalms by a variety of authors, sometimes named in the first line.

The Bible also describes David as a *harp* player (Amos 6:5), though the English word harp may be misleading. The word harp can translate two Hebrew words, *kinnor* and *nevel*.

The *kinnor* was a small instrument, probably about the size of a modern mandolin. According to Josephus (a Jewish historian writing in the 1st century A.D.) the ancient *kinnor* had ten strings attached to a bridge on a square soundbox. Two necks came out of each side of the soundbox, joined by a crossbar where the strings were attached. It was usually played with a pick.

No one's exactly sure what an ancient *nevel* was. Josephus wrote that it was a twelve-stringed instrument plucked by hand, but beyond that we don't know much. The word is related to "skin" or "skin-bottle." That might mean it was made out of animal skin. But it could also be a reference to a bottle-like shape. Most musicologists believe *nevel* strings went down from a crossbar directly into a soundbox, like a harp, but much smaller.[6]

FOUR

FINDING POWER TO FORGIVE

I
THE OASIS OF EIN GEDI

Next I need to chase David into the desert. As King Saul did. At first glance the Judean Desert is a vast emptiness, an arid, bleached, lonely space. There are few roads and fewer settlements. It's no wonder. Daytime temperatures can regularly top 100 degrees Fahrenheit, 38 Celsius. Vultures patrol the sky. Scorpions scuttle across the scorched sand. There's not a single Jerusalem bagel vendor in sight.

Can't wait to explore it.

✻   ✻   ✻

On my visit to the Judean Desert I take a bus south from Jerusalem. I look out the window to my left and see the western shore of the Dead Sea, the lowest spot on the face of the earth. Despite its name, it's actually a picturesque lake, pastel shades of green, blue, and yellow shimmering in the desert sun. Its beauty must have tempted and taunted parched travelers for centuries.

The furnace-like heat of the desert intensifies thirst into a kind of madness, yet the Dead Sea is so saturated with salt that it nourishes nothing. No fish or birds or other animals have ever adapted to it. Drink from this water and your thirst just gets worse; in fact, it will kill you. Yet as we roll along its shores, I wonder how many dehydrated wanderers just weren't able to resist the lure.

Off to my right, the sea is bordered by reddish mountains that rise sharply off the desert plain and seem to stretch to the sky. But as one desert guide puts it, "This is the only place in the world where you can climb cliffs 1,200 feet to their summit... and still be below sea level."[1]

As I look more closely at the cliffs I see entrances to dozens of deep *wadis*, Arabic for ravine. They form a maze of twisting canyons sliced into the desert plateau by winter floods over the centuries. Most of the year these ravines are bone dry, but one has been blessed with a resource that in this land is more precious than gold—continuous, clear, cool water.

It's easy to find now because of the signs directing traffic to park headquarters, but for thousands of years this *wadi* hid its life-giving secret, disguised from the outside as just another dry gulch. But inside? It's a lush oasis. The ancient name for this place is *Ein Gedi*, "Spring of the Mountain Goats." This is where I need to hike next if I'm going to stay on the trail of King David.

ISLAND IN THE SAND

Unlike most other places I'll visit on my David quest, Ein Gedi has changed very little since his day. Park rangers have cleared paths, but that's about as far as the modern world intrudes. Here, more than any other place on my journey, I am time-traveling into a world similar to the one David saw and felt and heard and smelled and tasted.

I get here early in the morning, before the crowds arrive on their tour buses. I want a chance to experience the emptiness. It's my first day on David's trail without a guide (Yeah, who needs a guide when hiking in the deepest desert on earth?). I hadn't seen a tree for miles while on the bus ride here, but a hundred yards into the canyon I'm in a forest. Another few minutes of hiking and my face is refreshed by cool spray from spring-fed waterfalls cascading into pools the color of jade.

I'm not the only creature enjoying the shade. Swallows, martins, and other small birds flit from tree to tree and fill the air with chirps and whistles. I turn the corner and almost walk right into a relaxed group of ibex, mountain goats with frighteningly huge curled horns. I look up to see amusing little hyraxes hanging out in the tree branches, fuzzy critters resembling teddy bears that lounge around napping for most of their lives.

The surrounding desert is life-threatening. But in the oasis, the livin' is easy.

It stays relatively cool here too, because tall canyon walls rise steeply on both sides, shading the ravine nearly all day long. I look up at the red, brown, and yellow cliffs and see dark dots—the entrances of cave after cave. I clamber into one of them, and the temperature drops another several degrees.

The four freshwater springs of Ein Gedi are so productive that even here, in the middle of the lowest desert on the planet, waterfalls flow year-round, 800 million gallons of water a year pouring into the natural pools of this canyon. Plants from tropical, Mediterranean, and desert climates abound—date palms, sugar cane, and beautiful flowers too, including one of the rarest orchids in the world. The atmosphere is almost Hawaiian. In fact, this small ravine has the densest concentration of tropical plants in Israel. It's a lush island of life, surrounded not by water but by sand.

II
ON THE RUN

It's becoming clear to me why David hid *here*. On the run from King Saul, David was accumulating a following. Those 400 destitute men who found him at Adullam are slowly being forged into skilled hunters, trackers, and warriors—and attracting others like them. David no longer needs a hideout just for himself. He needs a place where hundreds of his followers can find shelter, food, and water, and can disappear in an instant, melting into the rocks and caves without a trace. He found it all in this place.

For a while, at least, he must have felt some relief.

Then one day Saul gets wind of the fact that David's hiding here and probably thinks, *I've got him trapped.*

After Saul returned from fighting the Philistines, he was told that David had gone into the wilderness of Ein Gedi.

*So Saul chose 3,000 elite troops from all Israel and went to
search for David and his men...*

1 SAMUEL 24:1,2A NLT

Ein Gedi is lush, but it's also a box canyon. Once you're
inside, there are few ways out. Then Saul has to answer the call
of nature (The Bible is so real here—I watched six seasons of 24
and apparently Jack Bauer never had to relieve himself once.). He
happens to squat in the same cave where David's hiding. David's
men can't believe their good fortune. They urge him, *This is the
moment, boss! Sneak up and kill him right now and all our troubles
will be over!*

David says no.

How in the world is he able to resist solving his problem
once and for all with a convenient murder?

What David does next is a major shift from the way people
thought at the time—and often still think today. Unusual for
the violent, dog-eat-dog world of the Late Bronze Age Collapse,
David supports the rule of law vs. personal vengeance and honor
killing. At great cost to himself, he refuses to kill Saul—because
it would be murder. It's as if he's saying, these long centuries of
post-apocalyptic madness are coming to an end. I am drawing
the line. Civilization is making a comeback. Even if it makes life
harder for me.

✦   ✦   ✦

DIGGING DEEPER

SMELL LIKE AN EGYPTIAN

A thousand years after David, Ein Gedi became a surprising source of spectacular wealth. The world's most expensive perfume was produced with oil derived from a rare species of fragrant balsam tree that grew here—and only here.

This Ein Gedi perfume was known to be Cleopatra's favorite fragrance. When her lover Marc Anthony wanted to give the Egyptian queen a generous gift, he didn't just give her a bottle of the stuff. He confiscated the entire region of Ein Gedi so she could have a personal monopoly on the ingredients that produced the perfume. From that time on, only she could wear the fragrance. It was Chanel Number YOU CAN'T HAVE IT.

The exact identity of the balsam species that produced the essential oil for this perfume has been lost; most experts believe it to be extinct. No plant remaining in Ein Gedi matches descriptions of this fragrant "balsam" by ancient writers like Pliny the Elder. And believe me, I looked.

So, sorry. You will never smell like Cleopatra.

*

There are so many ways people can hurt us. They can take things from us, do things to us, speak badly about us. When that happens, our first instinct, and probably our constant daydream, is to hurt them back. In fact, our culture encourages us to get even. Or at least to nurse resentments. As Reese Witherspoon's character, Madeline Mackenzie, put it in the TV show *Big Little Lies*, "I love my grudges. I tend to them like little pets."

But a 2019 report in the Journal of Psychology and Aging found that holding grudges is dangerous to your health. Remaining in a state of anger is associated with chronic inflammation and other illnesses.[2] The effect intensifies with age; in other words, the longer you hold a grudge, the sicker you get. (Interestingly, in the same study, sadness showed no correlation with disease. Being sad is not unhealthy. Holding grudges is.) Dr. Frederic Luskin, founder of the Stanford Forgiveness Project, told the New York Times that unforgiveness "...shuts down and dampens immune response, leads to some aspects of depression... dysregulates the nervous system, (and) is the most harmful emotion for the cardiovascular system."[3]

So how can you do what's healthiest for you—and truly forgive, deep down, no matter what's been done to you? How can you do right when you've been wronged?

III
STEPS TO FORGIVENESS

David takes four steps to forgiveness. And each is crucial. Leave one out, and the four-dimensional picture of true biblical forgiveness gets dangerously skewed. These are the four equal sides of a holistic forgiveness that is truly soul-healing.

1. SEE THE BIGGER PICTURE

David's men are focused on the moment—*kill him now!* David sees a bigger picture. There is a bigger God with a bigger plan—and a bigger law against this.

What about you and me? What are we supposed to do when we are in David's situation— someone is hounding us, making life miserable? Most of us are unlikely to encounter foes trying to kill us, but people may intentionally or unintentionally harm us in other ways.

We too are subject to a bigger law, a command from Jesus himself. Are you ready for the hardest principle in the Bible to live by?

> *"But I tell you, love your enemies and pray for those who persecute you."*
>
> MATTHEW 5:44 NIV

Jesus practiced this. Peter, who watched Jesus tortured, gives us an eyewitness account:

> *When they hurled their insults at him, he did not retaliate; when he suffered, he made no threats. Instead, he entrusted himself to him who judges justly.*
>
> 1 PETER 2:23 NIV

That last phrase is key. *Entrust yourself to Him who judges justly.* This is what David does in verse 15:

> *"May the LORD be our judge and decide between us. May he consider my cause and uphold it; may he vindicate me by delivering me from your hand."*
>
> 1 SAMUEL 24:15 NIV

David is able to control himself because he trusts that there is a bigger plan, and ultimately a bigger God is in control. As he writes in Psalm 37:7–11:

> *Do not fret when people succeed in their ways,*
>   *when they carry out their wicked schemes.*
> *Refrain from anger and turn from wrath;*
>   *do not fret—it leads only to evil.*

I love that line. *"Refrain from anger and turn from wrath; do not fret—it leads only to evil."* Memorize that and make it a life value. You'll benefit from improved mental and physical health, as all those studies show. Anger and fretting lead only to evil. He continues:

> *For those who are evil will be destroyed,*
>   *but those who hope in the LORD will inherit the land.*
> *A little while, and the wicked will be no more;*
>   *though you look for them, they will not be found.*
> *But the meek will inherit the land*
>   *and enjoy peace and prosperity.*

David believes that, in the big picture, the wicked will not prosper, and the meek will. This is his worldview, enabling him to say, "I won't take this into my hands; I will leave it in the hands of God and the law."

Of course the rule of law also means you can use the law to seek justice, an option not available to David when he was on the run like this. I urge you, when you can, use legal means to seek justice. Just be sure you're using the law to seek *justice*, and not *vengeance*.

2. SHOW GRACE

Even though Saul's been trying to kill him, David does not harm Saul in that cave. What he does instead is so clever, so ingenious. He quietly cuts off a corner of Saul's garment—while Saul is, uh... focused on another task—and then later, when Saul is on the other side of the canyon, David holds up that piece of Saul's robe in order to prove his intentions. No mere words could better prove David's heart. With that piece of fabric as evidence, he says,

> *"Why do you listen when men say, 'David is bent on harming you'? This day you have seen with your own eyes how the LORD delivered you into my hands in the cave. Some urged me to kill you, but I spared you; I said, 'I will not lay my hand on my lord, because he is the LORD's anointed.' See, my father, look at this piece of your robe in my hand! I cut off the corner of your robe but did not kill you."*
>
> 1 SAMUEL 24:9–11A NIV

Don't miss this. David didn't just walk away reluctantly with his resentment intact. He didn't just stew silently in the cave while watching Saul go to the bathroom. He shows mercy. He demonstrates powerfully that he could have killed Saul, but didn't. His forgiveness is not just a passive act. It's proactive, powerful, personal.

Okay, but how do you and I do this? Look for ways to love and bless your enemies. If an in-person expression of forgiveness feels inappropriate or impossible, then intercede for them in prayer. Forgive them even if they never apologize. Refuse to spread gossip. These are not the acts of weak people; only strong people can substitute the natural tendency to attack with acts of mercy. When you show mercy, you're not just "letting bygones be bygones." You are initiating something positive.

And this is not a one-time thing for David. In chapter 26 he again has a chance to kill Saul. He sneaks into camp while Saul is asleep, steals his spear, and in the morning yells across the ravine, "Hey Saul, some bodyguard you've got. Look who has your spear! Me! I could have killed you but I showed you grace. Again."

That brings me to the really tough part of this story. If this were a Hollywood movie, David's demonstration of love for Saul would melt his adversary's heart. But this is real life. Saul... never changes! He repents temporarily but always reverts to his old murderous self. This is a story about showing grace to someone who hurts you—and never stops.

> His forgiveness is not just a passive act. It's pro-active, powerful, personal.

Mercy is not easy. It is not always rewarded. Sometimes the rewards come years later. Sometimes never. But actions of peace are important for several reasons:[4]

- They provide a positive outlet for feelings that could otherwise turn to bitterness.

- They remind you that you have a destiny greater than an endless cycle of reciprocation and anger. You have a higher calling.

- They help your enemies see that you are serious about your faith in God.

- They declare plainly to the world that God's kingdom operates on different principles than the kingdoms of this world.

- They draw people to the Son of David, Jesus, who forgave and blessed his enemies.

But how do you proactively show mercy when your enemies never stop being mean? David's response has two more elements that are necessary for your recovery, your safety, and your mental health.

3. SPEAK TRUTH

Even when you show grace to someone, you can still confront them with the truth of their actions. You don't have to suffer in silence. In fact, speaking the truth in love to someone is an act of grace. It may be that your reality check will bring them to their senses. And of course you must speak truth to authorities in the case of crime or abuse. Speaking truth about the harm done to you does not mean you haven't forgiven. David shouts across the ravine, in a voice loud enough for everyone to hear:

> *"See that there is nothing in my hand to indicate that I am guilty of wrongdoing or rebellion. I have not wronged you, but you are hunting me down to take my life. May the LORD judge between you and me. And may the LORD avenge the wrongs you have done to me, but my hand will not touch you."*
>
> 1 SAMUEL 24:11B–12 NIV

David forgives—but he has the strength to speak truth to Saul. Forgiveness does not mean you look the other way. It does not mean you say it's okay. It does not mean you justify what the other person is doing. It does not mean you don't testify to authorities. You can forgive—but still speak truth.

And there's one more very important step to forgiveness that, in my observation, many Christians never take.

4. STAY SAFE

Forgive. But stay safe! Saul says, in essence, *Oh David, I am so so so sorry. I will never do it again. I am leaving; now please come with me.*

Does David *forgive* him? Yes. Does David *trust* him? Not for one second. In fact, he never trusts Saul again. Watch this:

> *"Then Saul returned home, but David and his men went up to the stronghold."*
>
> 1 SAMUEL 24:22 NIV

The Hebrew word for "stronghold" in that verse is *masada*. It means "strong foundation or support; refuge; fortress." Some scholars suspect David and his men went to the place known since ancient times as Masada, a plateau close to Ein Gedi, towering about 1,300 feet above the desert floor. Shaped like a giant ocean liner, this mesa was protected by sheer cliffs on every side.

Why would David and his men leave Ein Gedi while Saul's army retreats? *They do not trust him.* At the *masada*, a sneak attack would be impossible due to the deep drop on every side. And at this height, David could observe Saul and his troops for miles. He wants to see if Saul really leaves.

David does not go back home, arms around Saul's shoulders, ready to play him more of those harp riffs he loves so much and enjoy some Jerusalem bagels together. He has no way of knowing if Saul's repentance is real. He will not put himself in harm's way again with this unreliable, unstable, abusive man.

There is a difference between grace and gullibility. There is a difference between forgiveness and trust. You *have* to forgive people. The Bible commands it. You *don't* have to trust them. Forgiveness, by definition, is *given*. It is not earned or deserved. Trust *must* be earned.

> There is a difference between grace and gullibility. There is a difference between forgiveness and trust.

David understands this with crystal clarity. I hope you do too. Like David, you may need to hide in a stronghold of safety even as you forgive the one harming you.

IV
THE FORGIVENESS MIRACLE

Before we leave the desert, I want to encourage you. I know this is hard.

To you, the David and Saul story may sound more like a fairy tale than the David and Goliath story. You can imagine yourself defeating a physically superior opponent. But forgive that person who tried to ruin your life? That seems impossible.

Maybe it is, in a human sense. Maybe it would take a miracle.

But I believe in miracles. I've seen at least one.

Dan and Lynn Wagner attend the church I pastor. They were driving their Ford Aerostar mini-van home from a Christian music festival on the beach when an SUV ran a stop sign at 50 miles per hour and smashed into them from the left, instantly killing their only children, teenage daughters Mandie and Carrie, and severely injuring Dan and Lynn. The driver of the SUV, a woman named Lisa, was both drunk and high on drugs. Her own children, two and three years old, were with her in the car.

It's been over a decade since the accident and incredibly Lisa and Lynn now speak at events together, sharing their story of forgiveness and love. Lynn has become one of Lisa's closest advisors and encouragers.

But this miracle of forgiveness didn't happen overnight.

"Forgiving Lisa was a process," Lynn tells me as we sit together in the Wagner living room. I look over her shoulder and see a painting of the girls by a local artist, done from a photograph after their death, hanging on one wall. It's as if Mandie and Carrie are supporting their mom as she continues. "Lisa was 'that terrible woman' for a very long time," Lynn admits. "My first thought every morning was, *that woman*... But somewhere along the line we felt compassion for her."

"When Lisa went off to prison," Dan explains, "we began to feel something for her, to grieve for her. Because here was another woman losing her children, in her case for the duration of her sentence."

So they began to see her as a human being and not as a monster. But how did they get to the point of *forgiving* Lisa? "I really wanted the joy of life back," explains Lynn. "I knew if I kept swallowing that unforgiveness, it would be just like drinking poison that I hoped would kill her. Because I was still mad at her. But it would only poison my system."

Then there was another reason. "Slowly I realized that forgiving is not optional. God tells us to forgive." Lynn looks me in the eye to make her point with quiet insistence. "That's because He knows it's for our own benefit. When you have unforgiveness, you're chained to that person. You drag them around with you. I think we all know people who rehearse and rehearse their bitterness, and that's no way to live."

Dan is eager to clarify. "That does not absolve the other person. It doesn't mean you forget about what happened. It doesn't mean the pain goes away. It just means that emotionally you are free. And not just emotionally. There are a lot of physical issues that go along with unforgiveness."

> When you have unforgiveness, you're chained to that person. You drag them around with you.

What helped him the most through the process? "My journey to forgiveness was really helped along by digging into the Word. I read through the New Testament over and over, and God really softened my heart," Dan says.

Lynn leans forward and softly insists, "But I would tell anyone who needs to forgive to be gentle on themselves. Take time. It's a process. Seek somebody who can help you, someone who can walk alongside you when you're going through heavy stuff."

"A blessing has come out of this for me," she says with a smile. "Loving Lisa, encouraging Lisa, seeing her growth. That is the blessing for me."

Incredible? I know what I see when I look into their eyes. I see souls refreshed by living water, and not dried up by a spiritual desert.

TAKE TIME TO PROCESS

I want to reemphasize what Lynn said. It can take time. You may not be able to forgive instantly.

You know what? David couldn't forgive instantly, either. His actions were the end result of a process, of many long nights when he cried out to God in pain.

How do I know? You saw his thought process in those cave psalms already. You can see it in several other psalms too. He expresses anger, agony, and anxiety: anger about the past, agony in the present, and anxiety about the future.

Here's a sample. This is David verbally processing his pain:

They plot injustice and say,
> *"We have devised a perfect plan!"*
But God will shoot them with his arrows;
> *they will suddenly be struck down.*

> PSALM 64:6A,7 NIV

The enemy pursues me,
> *he crushes me to the ground;*
he makes me dwell in the darkness like those long dead.
So my spirit grows faint within me;
> *my heart within me is dismayed...*
In your unfailing love, silence my enemies;
> *destroy all my foes!*

> PSALM 143:3,4,12A NIV

He deeply feels these emotions. He doesn't try to pretend it's easy. He asks God to avenge these wrongs. Being honest about your emotions, as David was, is an important part of the process. But David doesn't camp out in the heat of his bitterness forever. Something else begins to capture his imagination.

V
THE SECRET OF WONDER

Later that evening I stand outside my hotel on the shore of the Dead Sea. The Jordanian mountains on the other side reflect the burnt-orange glow of the dying sunset behind me. Soon the light fades and a sliver of moon becomes visible in the darkening sky, a bright planet dangling beneath it. Then as if on cue, thousands of stars reveal their own light, their majesty far more visible here in the desert than in the city-lit skies at home, more beautiful and vast than I could ever take in. I keep looking as my eyes adjust and I see more and more tiny blossoms of light.

It suddenly strikes me that these same stars looked down on David and Saul 30 centuries ago. And I have a glimmer of the big-picture insight that motivated David in his best moments. If you're struggling to show grace to someone, try David's method. First he vents. But eventually he doesn't even really think about Saul anymore. Or the conflict. He focuses instead on God.

He runs to the refuge. And he sees the stars:

> *Your unfailing love, O LORD, is as vast as the heavens;*
> *your faithfulness reaches beyond the clouds.*
>
> PSALM 36:5 NLT

Look up. Find security in how much the Creator God loves you and remains faithful to you. For David, that's the real oasis:

> *All humanity finds shelter*
> *in the shadow of your wings.*
> *You feed them from the abundance of your own house,*
> *letting them drink from your river of delights.*

For you are the fountain of life,
the light by which we see.

PSALM 36:7–9 NLT

David's wonder at God's love lifts his gaze past the desert danger and the killer-king to the star-starter, the grace-giver, the cosmos-creator. Awe is his antidote to anger.

God's grace can be a place of life-giving refreshment for you too. As Brennan Manning says, "We should be astonished at the goodness of God, stunned that He should bother to call us by name, our mouths wide open at His love, bewildered that at this very moment we are standing on holy ground."[5]

> Awe is his antidote to anger.

You have access to the oasis. Living in awe of his grace helps you move past the bitterness. Because how you give grace to others is largely based on how much you grasp the grace given you, how much you embrace the love that envelops you.

RESIST THE DEAD SEA

When someone has done you wrong, the desire for justice can be intensified into a kind of madness. It gets to the point where it feels so necessary and so righteous to recount your grievance, again and again.

You even begin to thirst for it, for the daily opportunity to remind yourself and others of how badly you've been mistreated. You keep visiting that sea of bitterness, where nothing can live. Every time you remember the wrong done to you, every time you drink from the water of grievance, it feels a little like justice, because the wrong is neither overlooked nor forgotten! But while it shimmers and entices, ultimately that salty sea nourishes nothing. Drink from that water and your thirst just gets worse. In fact, it'll kill you. Yet so many wounded travelers just can't resist the lure. And slowly their souls shrivel.

Instead, look for the oasis. The refuge. Refresh your soul under the waterfall of God's grace. That's where life is found, even in the desert.

So far we've seen David make himself at home in shepherd's fields and battlefields, caves and canyons. But the most elusive destination for David remains the promised throne. And that remained the most elusive place for archaeologists to trace, too. Until one maverick scholar dug where no one else had dared. ✿

DIGGING DEEPER

SURPRISING DESERT

The Dead Sea region holds plenty of surprises for those expecting a lifeless, sun-scorched wilderness.

No Sunburn

This is probably the only desert on earth where you can sunbathe for extended periods with little or no sunburn. Harmful ultraviolet rays are filtered through three layers. Since it's about 1,200 feet below sea level, the atmosphere is so thick that fewer UVB rays get through. The ozone layer is also unusually robust here. And there's an additional evaporation layer that always hangs above the Dead Sea, filtering even more sunlight.

Tiny Elephant Cousins

The hyraxes that hang out on rocks and tree branches here look like mellow bunnies with rounded ears, but zoologists say they're actually related to the elephant. Their skeletons reveal the resemblance. The hyraxes also have tusks (though tiny) and similar feet.

Living Zoo

There are more elusive creatures here too. Leopards, striped hyenas, wolves, two types of foxes, and porcupines tend to hide from humans, but you can sometimes find their paw prints and scat on the paths. All life in the desert finds refuge in the oasis.

FIVE

FINDING HOPE WHEN DREAMS DIE

2 SAMUEL 7

I
JAFFA GATE, JERUSALEM

Today I finally track David out of the wilderness and into his Jerusalem palace.

On this February morning I'm bundled up against a chill in the air. The sky threatens rain. Most Western tourists imagine weather in the Middle East as an unbroken string of blisteringly hot days, so they're often surprised when a visit to Jerusalem requires a raincoat.

I climb stone steps to the ancient Jaffa Gate, a castle-like tower guarding the western side of the Old City where Danny Herman has arranged to meet me. Right outside the gate an old Arab vendor sells fresh Jerusalem bagels from a tray balanced expertly on a large cardboard box. On a damp morning like this they're almost irresistible, but I've been gorging myself on super-sweet Middle Eastern desserts every night and I know I should just look the other way. I buy two.

"Boker Tov, René!" I hear the Hebrew for "good morning" behind me, and turn to see Danny dressed in a hat, scarf, sweater, and down jacket. I offer him one of my bagels as if I'd planned it—and we're off.

THE REAL CITY OF DAVID

Danny takes me to the edge of the stone platform in front of the Jaffa Gate and sweeps his arm in a grand circle to indicate the buildings that surround us. "Over there, King David Hotel. On King David Street. Behind us, the Citadel of David. Also known as David's Tower. Just around that corner, the Tomb of David. When all this was named, everyone thought this was the part of town where David had lived." He pauses for emphasis. "They were all wrong! No evidence of David's city here at all. Zero! But! Now we have archaeological, scientific evidence that David's Jerusalem was on the other side of this hill! Let's go!"

Before I know it he's ten paces ahead of me, through the gate and plunging into the Arab *souk*, the maze of cobbled streets that comprise the ancient market of the Old City. I race to catch up and we stride past colorful stalls heaped with hookahs, layered with lamps, piled with pots. We burst into an open plaza. I look to my left and see the famous Western Wall of the Temple Mount, where thousands of Jews pray every day.

I slow down momentarily to take in the spectacle, then realize Danny's stride is unbroken and he's already across the plaza and halfway through the Dung Gate. I bolt ahead (wondering briefly why it's named "Dung Gate" and if I should be concerned) and we zoom through, across the street, down a block, and suddenly stop. Danny points to his left. "This is it. No place in the world will get you closer to David."

We are standing at the entrance to an archaeological site known as The City of David, on a narrow ridge jutting south from the Old City. Hidden underground here for centuries was the original core of Jerusalem, dating back at least 7,000 years. How these ruins were rediscovered is one of the most fascinating stories in archaeology.

II
THE TEMPLE MOUNT, JERUSALEM

It was a hot summer day in 1865.

Angela Burdett Coutts, a British woman on a pilgrimage to Jerusalem, was parched. Her guide Mahmoud brought her a bucket of water from a nearby well, but she found the smelly water barely drinkable. She wondered, *Would King David have imbibed such water?* Upon investigation she discovered that all drinking water in the city was being retrieved from stale cisterns contaminated by surface runoff; consequently, Jerusalem was plagued with disease. Surely, she reasoned, there were better sources of water here in ancient times.

On her return to England she organized a foundation, the Water Relief Committee, to find better water sources in Palestine.

She was able to almost instantly secure funds, hire staff, and receive a glowing public endorsement from Queen Victoria. Did I mention she was a British baroness, owned the largest private bank in England, was probably the richest woman in England, and enjoyed close friendships with influential celebrities including Charles Dickens? Using this considerable clout, Angela recruited the best civil engineers to help. The Water Relief Committee quickly broadened its scope to become the Palestine Exploration Fund, which still exists today.

Soon a globetrotting land surveyor named Charles Warren (the future head of Scotland Yard) was appointed to lead the exploration. According to some reports, Queen Victoria also gave him a secret mission: since you'll be underground anyway, she suggested, do some exploring. Find treasure if you can. And spy on the Ottoman government (which controlled Palestine at the time).

In 1867 Warren tried to dig on the Temple Mount itself, but was banned by the (rightly suspicious) Ottoman authorities. He then thought, *Okay, if I can't dig on the Temple Mount, I'll dig near the Temple Mount.* Warren settled in an area to the south, attempting first to secretly bore tunnels underneath the Temple area.

One winter day, water began to flow through his excavation. Warren followed the water to its source, the Gihon Spring. The spring was concealed under ancient stonework hundreds of yards south of the Temple Mount, at the foot of an unimpressive narrow ridge.

In that moment Warren had a flash of insight which upended the conventional geography of Jerusalem: any freshwater spring would have been the center of ancient development. David's city was likely *there*, on that nondescript hill outside the medieval city walls, *not* in the walled city to the north, which had no fresh water source.

After removing a mound of rubble, Warren found a dark shaft leading from the spring into the depths of the hill. Faced with a potentially unstable passageway unexplored for centuries and leading to unknown danger, Warren did what any self-respecting 19th century Victorian adventurer would do: he lit a torch and plunged in. He and a friend crawled through the winding channel.

Then Warren noticed the flame of his torch flickering. There was a draft coming from somewhere. He looked up and saw a tall, vertical crevice. He and his friend climbed the shaft, their backs to one side of the wall while their feet pushed against the other. At the top, they found it led to another manmade tunnel, then to another. This maze of tunnels and chambers, like levels in a video game, connected the spring, at the base of the hill, all the way to the hilltop.

While in these shafts, Warren remembered an obscure Bible verse: 2 Samuel 5:8 says David and his men climbed what's called a *tsinnor*, an archaic Hebrew word usually translated as "water shaft" or "drainpipe," to infiltrate and conquer the Jebusite city of Jerusalem. *Could this be that very shaft?* Warren's suspicions deepened. He would later write a book publicizing his theory that this forgotten hillside was the original location of David's Jerusalem.

But his theory wouldn't be confirmed for another 150 years.

✧   ✧   ✧

After we're stopped twice by security guards, Danny and I get special permission from the site supervisors at the City of David archaeological park to proceed on our own into the tunnels Warren discovered and film what we find. Starting at the top of the hill, we climb down into the ancient water system. I'm glad to be headed underground, because those ominous February storm clouds are starting to make good on their threat, drenching the city with cold rain.

About halfway through the underground passageway, as a few electric bulbs eerily illuminate the ancient tunnel walls, Danny turns toward me. "Wait," he says seriously. "I have something important for you to hear." He takes out his phone. Opens an app.

And soon I hear an mp3 of the "Raiders of the Lost Ark" theme echoing through the cavern.

But really, the soundtrack fits! After all, I'm with an archaeologist in a somewhat eerie subterranean chamber and as we wander around, Danny tells me quite seriously that no one is exactly sure how many tunnels there are down here—only that there are certainly more to be discovered.

Then Danny shares a story about a true archaeological superstar who made her name down here, a woman who took Warren's hunch about the location of David's city and ran with it. Piecing together forgotten clues, strange museum artifacts, and notes from her own grandfather's lifelong obsession, she went on a quest for David's palace. And she may have found it.

Danny continues the story as we clamber down.

THE PALACE PUZZLE

In 1936, Professor Benjamin Mazar became a celebrity archaeologist when he discovered the 1800-year-old forgotten tomb of Yehuda Hanasi, the legendary compiler of the *Mishnah*, the ancient collection of Jewish teachings. But his real interest was the area near the Temple Mount in Jerusalem. He dug there a few times himself, searching for something to confirm that this was the site of David's capital. But a decisive discovery eluded him.

The challenge facing any archaeologist in Jerusalem is that it's one of the world's oldest cities, going back thousands of years before David, and thousands of years after him. During all those centuries, older buildings were continually demolished to make way for the new; entire structures were dismantled, their pieces reused in later construction. That makes any excavation here like putting together a puzzle—with most pieces still missing.

Yet it was one of those puzzle pieces that stuck in Benjamin Mazar's mind as a possible clue. Digging here in the 1960s, British archaeologist Kathleen Kenyon found an oddity—the top of a beautiful five-foot-long column carved in proto-Aeolic, or Phoenician style. But the Phoenicians were an empire on the coast, far north of Jerusalem. What was a giant Phoenician-style column doing here?

DEATHBED INSIGHTS

Meanwhile, Benjamin's young granddaughter, Eilat, started hanging out with her grandpa on numerous summer digs. She became obsessed with his profession, and would eventually earn a doctorate in archaeology herself.

One night in 1995, visiting her ailing grandfather not long before he passed away, Dr. Eilat Mazar told him she had a hunch. She thought everyone looking for David's palace had been digging in the wrong place. She suspected it was a little further north, basing her suspicions on a Bible verse: 2 Samuel 5:17 says that David "went down" from his palace to his fortress.

The ancient fortress of Jerusalem had already been uncovered by archaeologists following Charles Warren's theory. The only spot on the ridge from which David could have "gone down" to the fortress was a slightly higher outcropping of rock hidden under a modern building. So, Eilat theorized, that's where the remains of his palace might be.

When she told her grandfather her idea, he leaned forward, eyes twinkling with excitement. "Wait, Ellie. Think! Where, exactly, did Kathleen Kenyon find the top of that Phoenician-style column? Wasn't it right next to the place you're talking about?" She ran to her grandfather's library to check Kenyon's reports and realized he was right.

He then reminded her of another Bible verse, one describing the crew David hired to build his palace. The Bible says he made an arrangement with the Phoenician king to use his skilled architects and artisans (2 Samuel 5:11). "Ellie," Benjamin said, "Phoenician workers would have constructed his palace in their style—not Israelite style. *Exactly the style of the piece Kenyon found!* I think if you could dig there, you may indeed find David's palace!"

CLUES UNEARTHED

After waiting ten more years for permission to dig, Eilat began excavations in mid-February 2005, keeping her suspicions to herself. Almost immediately, her team found giant walls between six and eight feet wide extending in every direction beyond the site. More evidence emerged: imported luxury goods, including two Phoenician-style ivory decorations and several finely crafted round bowls, supporting both a tenth century date and a sophisticated, urban lifestyle. A bone was radiocarbon-dated to show a probable date between 1050 and 780 B.C.[1]

Her conclusions about the building she found? "Archaeologically, it appears that it was built either slightly before or slightly after 1000 B.C.E., about when the Bible tells us King

David conquered Jerusalem," she wrote in an archaeological journal. "The Biblical narrative, I submit, better explains the archaeology we have uncovered than any other hypothesis that has been put forward. Indeed, the archaeological remains square perfectly with the Biblical description."[2]

Remember, this is not a pastor or a rabbi, but a respected scientist—arguably the leader in her field—making conclusions based on evidence.

I ask Danny what he thinks. "I want to make it clear," he says, "We don't have a doormat saying, 'Welcome To My Palace, from King David!' But the circumstantial evidence—the Proto-Aeolic Capital, some of the pottery, the shape of the architecture, all of this seems to suggest, this is it, René. This could be the corner of David's palace. I totally trust Dr. Mazar's opinion because she is really an expert on the Iron Age."

So while research on the site continues, the lead scholar's working theory is that this was probably the royal palace of David. As I stand in the very spot where David may have ruled, I picture the next episode in his story.

III
DREAM DENIED

David's life now enters a whole series of plot twists. Ready for the ride? In ten short chapters (1 Samuel 27–2 Samuel 5), this happens:

Bad news: David and his men foolishly decide to fight as mercenaries for their erstwhile enemies the Philistines. Then their king demands that David fight against Israel!

Good news: When the other Philistine commanders say they don't trust David, he's sent back to his home base of Ziklag.

Bad news: When he gets home, he discovers it's been sacked by Amalekites, who have stolen everything and kidnapped the women and children.

Good news: David goes in hot pursuit and after an adventure gets everything back.

Bad news: Meanwhile, Saul and Jonathan die in battle. David laments them.

Good news: David finally becomes king over the southernmost tribes of Judah and Benjamin at age 30, coronated in the city of Hebron.

But wait! Bad news: One of Saul's sons, Ish-bosheth, names himself king over the rest of Israel. Civil war ensues.

Good news: David's men win.

Bad news: After the war ends, two of Ish-bosheth's men kill him while he sleeps. They assume David will celebrate, but instead he has them executed for murder.

Good news: Finally David begins his 33-year reign over the united 12 tribes of Israel (after already ruling in Hebron for seven years over the two southern tribes). He celebrates with a bagel.

Whew. It's enough plot for another phase of the Marvel Cinematic Universe. And I didn't even tell you about the witch or the séance (1 Samuel 28).

Okay. David is now firmly in control in Jerusalem, so how is he going to get these twelve squabbling tribes of Israel truly unified under his monarchy?

The clock is ticking. The Philistines are regrouping. If the Israelites don't unite soon, they'll be picked off by a stronger foe. But they are suspicious of one another, difficult to lead, fiercely independent.

David has a two-step plan.

Step one: Move the capital from Hebron to Jerusalem. Why Jerusalem? Neutral ground. The ancestor of all twelve tribes, Abraham, had worshipped God there. Yet Jerusalem had never belonged to any Israelite tribe; it's essentially neutral territory. That makes it the perfect place for the new capital.

Small wrinkle. It's already occupied by a feisty people called the Jebusites. They're so cocky about their city's seeming invulnerability that they shout down from their walls at David's men, "Our blind and lame could defend our city against you!" I'm sure the blind and lame really appreciated that.

But before the echoes of those boasts fade, David's wilderness-tested men shimmy up a water channel (as Charles Warren remembered, this is the most likely translation of the Hebrew tsinnor) and promptly plant their flag in the middle of town. "Uh, what were you saying about your invulnerable fortress?"

Yet David treats these Jebusites mercifully. He spares their lives and even, when he wants some of their land to build a temple, buys it at full price rather than just taking it outright (1 Chronicles 21:24). They apparently join his people as allies (Zechariah 9:7).

DIGGING DEEPER

WHAT'S WITH THE HEBREWS?

When David offers his men as mercenaries to the Philistine king, some of the king's military commanders protest, "What are these Hebrews doing here?" Today the word "Hebrew" is used mostly to refer to the Jewish language. But the origin of the word is a great story illuminated by archaeology.

The Bible usually describes the twelve tribes descended from Jacob as "Israelites" or "Children of Israel" (the term "Jew" developed centuries later, during the Babylonian exile; a person is first described as "Jewish" in the Book of Esther, around 550 B.C.). The term used by the Philistines, "Hebrews" (ivrim in the Hebrew language), is used in the Bible only in places where non-Israelites, like Egyptians or Philistines, are speaking about Israelites, or when Israelites are distinguishing themselves from non-Israelites. In other words, it was the word recognized by outsiders to identify Israelites.

But what does it mean? It may be related to the word habiru, found in ancient Mesopotamian archives at Mari, a site in modern Syria. In these tablets habiru is a general description of raiders who were plundering towns. Then that word gets applied to a specific group of people by the Canaanites around 1200 B.C. Archaeologists uncovered references to a people called the Habiru in Egyptian clay tablets found at a site called Tell el-Amarna. The tablets included intelligence reports from Canaanites informing their Egyptian overlords about these Habiru, newly arrived tribes bent on conquest.[3] The timeline fits the Bible descriptions of the Hebrew journey into Canaan perfectly.

So the term "Hebrew" may be an instance of people taking an insult ("what are these brigands, these raiders, doing here?") and proudly adopting it as their own.

Now that he has his neutral-territory capital, it's time for Step Two: Unite all the tribes around worship of the one God, Yahweh. To do that, David plans to bring the great reminder of their shared national story of deliverance, the Ark of the Covenant, into his capital city. The 400-year-old Ark is the holy chest containing Moses' stone tablets of God's law. After a false start, the priests bring the Ark into the city with an impressive parade. David himself leads the procession, dancing in ecstatic celebration. And you're going to think I am making this up, but to mark the occasion he gives everyone in the crowd a fun commemorative meal consisting of a raisin cake, a date cake, and... Jerusalem bread!

Obviously the ark couldn't yet be placed in the Jerusalem temple; that building wouldn't exist until Solomon, David's son, constructed it 37 years later. So David readies temporary digs, apparently a tent similar to the Tabernacle.

This troubles David. He's living in luxury, in that stone-and-cedar palace built by the Phoenicians for him, while the Ark's still in a tent. So he tells Nathan the prophet, "I'm going to build a temple for the Lord and for the Ark to reside in."

Nathan says, "Great idea."

But that night Nathan receives a message from God. To his surprise, God says no to David's dream of building the temple.

"Go and tell my servant David, This is what the LORD has declared: 'Are you the one to build a house for me to live in? I have never lived in a house... I have never once complained... I have never asked, "Why haven't you built me a beautiful cedar house?"'

2 SAMUEL 7:5–7 NLT

Did I ask for a temple? Did I give you this job? Do I seem unhappy?
And then God reminds David about his grace toward him:

> "*I took you from the pasture, from tending the flock, and*
> *appointed you ruler over my people Israel. I have been*
> *with you wherever you have gone... Now I will make your*
> *name great, like the names of the greatest men on earth...*
> *the LORD himself will establish a house for you...*"
>
> 2 SAMUEL 7:8–11B NIV

So David starts the day by saying, "I want to build the Lord a
house," and God essentially says, "No thanks, but I'll build *you* a
house—that will last forever and ever!"

IV
HOW TO HANDLE IT WHEN GOD SAYS NO

How will David handle God's grace-filled but firm rejection of
His dream? After all, God wasn't slamming the door on a selfish
ambition. David's dream seemed a laudable goal.

But sometimes God just says no. Even to seemingly good
things. For reasons he may never disclose.

This is a very personal subject for me. I'll never forget the
very first time I taught on this passage, as pastor of a small church
at South Lake Tahoe, California. Laurie and I had been hoping
to conceive our first child, yet despite medical intervention it
just wasn't happening. There were a lot of tears and a lot of
frustration but finally we prayed, "God, we believe that, for
whatever reason, for right now, you are saying... *no.*"

What do you do when God says no to that pregnancy, no to that job, no to that college, no to that raise, no to that transfer, no to that marriage, no to that adoption, no to that healing?

I was scheduled to speak on this very passage that week. Can you imagine how relevant it seemed? In my sermon that Sunday, I shared from my heart how Laurie and I were moved by David's response to God. I told them how we believed God was saying no to us. And how we found a model for our response in David's own prayer. I've had to revisit that conviction many times.

As I told the congregation that day, David chooses to focus on four aspects of God's character that he knows are true:

1. GOD IS GRACIOUS

David reflects on God's undeserved grace toward him:

> *"Who am I, Sovereign LORD, and what is my family, that you have brought me this far?"*
>
> 2 SAMUEL 7:18 NLT

God has blessed him with so much already that he does not deserve.

> *"What more can I say to you? You know what your servant is really like, Sovereign LORD."*
>
> 2 SAMUEL 7:20 NLT

Interesting phrasing. *You know what your servant is really like.*

In case you find yourself put off at times by David's violence, particularly when he is younger and fighting the Philistines, here he seems to be having a similar reaction when he looks back at his own life. In First Chronicles, when David tells his son Solomon this story, he adds a telling detail:

> "*...this word of the LORD came to me: 'You have shed much blood and have fought many wars. You are not to build a house for my Name, because you have shed much blood on earth in my sight.'*"
>
> 1 CHRONICLES 22:8

In fact David seems astounded that, despite his past questionable actions, God still has mercy on him. In essence he's saying, "God, you are saying no to this dream, but I can't complain. I already have so much I do not deserve. If I never received another thing from you I'm already richly blessed, just to have your mercy. Just to be alive!"

2. GOD HAS BLESSED

Sometimes when God says no, all I focus on is what I didn't get. In times like that, I need to redirect my thoughts away from what I *want* and toward what I *already have*. David thinks of the great things God has already done for him:

> "*And as if this were not enough in your sight, Sovereign LORD, you have also spoken about the future of the house of your servant—and this decree, Sovereign LORD, is for a mere human!*"
>
> 2 SAMUEL 7:19 NIV

He remembers not just personal blessings, but also the blessings God has given to the people of Israel throughout history:

*"And who is like your people Israel—the one nation on
earth that God went out to redeem as a people for himself,
and to make a name for himself, and to perform great and
awesome wonders by driving out nations and their gods
from before your people, whom you redeemed from Egypt?
You have established your people Israel as your very own
forever, and you, LORD, have become their God."*

2 SAMUEL 7:23,24 NIV

Again, he is remembering
chosenness, both his own and
his nations's.

You can do the same
thing. Recall past blessings
on your life, on your family,
on your country. Most of all,
remind yourself what God has
done for you, and for all who trust in Him through Christ.

> The word *no* can
> be one of God's
> best gifts to you.

3. GOD IS GOOD

When I am told *no* by God, I find it helpful to reaffirm my trust in
God's essential goodness. God is still good. Even when God says
no. This is really where David's going when he says:

*"How great you are, Sovereign LORD! There is no one like
you, and there is no God but you..."*

2 SAMUEL 7:22 NIV

There is no God but you. There's a little exercise I occasionally
lead our congregation in during worship services at church.
Everyone points their fingers upward and says, "God." Then they

point to themselves and say, "Not." Try it yourself. God. Not. *Repeat as necessary.*

The point: He rules, I don't. When I truly believe God is good and God is sovereign, I can do two things:

- **Thank God for his veto power.** The word *no* can be one of God's best gifts to you. Aren't you glad God has not answered all your prayers the way you wanted?

- **See "no" as redirection, not rejection.** Believe that God is using even this *no* for his purposes, purposes that maybe you will never see. Even if the door slammed in your face seems to stem from an unfair boss or an unjust situation or an incurable disease, even if it seems the *no* is not directly coming from God, He will still use the *no* for His purposes. He will still bring good out of it. His *no* today paves the way for a better *yes* tomorrow.

> God sees all of eternity; we can't even see into tomorrow.

And that leads right to the final acknowledgement David makes in his response to God:

4. GOD KNOWS BEST

The reason for God's *no* is because God *knows*. David trusts that God knows exactly what he and the people of Israel need. God sees the whole chess game; we can barely see one move at a time. God sees all of eternity; we can't even see into tomorrow.

And so David chooses to receive the blessing God has for him, rather than focus on the blessing he was denied:

"Sovereign LORD, you are God! Your covenant is trustworthy, and you have promised these good things to your servant. Now be pleased to bless the house of your servant, that it may continue forever in your sight; for you, Sovereign LORD, have spoken, and **with your blessing the house of your servant will be blessed forever.***"*

2 SAMUEL 7:28–29 NIV

Did you catch the wisdom in that last phrase? *"...with your blessing... your servant will be blessed..."* This is one of the most essential yet most elusive choices you and I can make: *Choose to be blessed with God's blessing.*

Can you pray David's prayer? *"With your blessing I will be blessed."*

> Choose to be blessed with God's blessing

Choose to be blessed with the blessing God has chosen for you. Who cares if others get other blessings? I guarantee you they also get other heartaches.

There's a crucial component to David's prayer that I don't want you to miss. Look at those two verses a little more closely. See all those words about the future, like *promised and forever*? He's saying, I choose to believe that, even though God said no to me *now*, he still has a great *future* for me and my family, guaranteed forever.

Can you believe that? That even though the desire you have isn't fulfilled (at least, not yet), you can still have a great life and great blessings and great impact—and that in the new heavens and new earth God's eternal blessings will outlast any disappointment here?

Here's the bottom line. Don't cling so hard to the dream you *want* that you miss the dream God is *giving you.*

You could summarize David's four points in a little rhyme. It may sound simple at first, but it's not simplistic:

God is gracious
God has blessed
God is good and
God knows best

A lot of deep truth in those simple words.

DIGGING DEEPER

KING SOLOMON'S MINES

It's long been a mystery: what was the source of David and Solomon's wealth? When Solomon finally built the Temple, the Bible says it was festooned with metal decorations. Where did they come from? University of Tel Aviv archaeologist Erez Ben-Yosef may have an answer. He began exploring an ancient copper mine in the desert south of Jerusalem in 2013. His team uncovered a several-acre smelting plant, with massive kilns where raw copper ore was superheated and turned into metal. More than 1,000 tons of slag, the waste material left after smelting, were found at the site, indicating industrial-level metal production at a scale no one previously suspected. Copper was extremely valuable, the oil of its day, according to experts.

But who operated the site, and when? Precise radio-carbon dating of piles of donkey dung found at the site indicates that its heyday was in the 10th century B.C.—precisely the time David and Solomon ruled as Israel's kings.[4] (And yes, I'd rather be a beer archaeologist than a dung archaeologist.)

Ben-Yosef told National Geographic, "Until recently we had almost nothing from this period in this area. Now we not only know that this was a source of copper, but also that it's from the days of King David and his son Solomon. There's a serious possibility that Jerusalem got its wealth from taxing these mining operations."[5]

V
THE YES AFTER EVERY NO

That first time I taught on this passage, when Laurie and I were struggling with infertility, I was very vulnerable with our congregation. I told them how God was saying no to our prayers for having children, and how we were really struggling—there had been so many tears and so much heartache—but we were learning to accept his answer.

Just a few days after that sermon we were delighted by the absolutely surprising news that we were expecting a baby. I got up in church the very next weekend and started my sermon by stammering, "Well...God said yes!"

> Don't cling so hard to the dream you want that you miss the dream God is giving you.

I didn't have to say another word. The entire congregation understood and erupted in cheers. Someone even got to their feet and started singing the old hymn, "Great Is Thy Faithfulness." One after another, others rose and joined in. It was incredibly moving. We cried and sang and laughed and rejoiced together in God's surprise.

Question: Why did God put us through all that time of *no* before there was a *yes*?

I don't know exactly—but I know this: I would not trade that moment of joy for anything. The times of *no* before the *yes* intensified our joy. Even more importantly, Laurie and I also both grew so much during that long time of frustration.

Here's an even harder question. Is every *no* you receive really God's perfect will? Let's be brutally, uncomfortably real here. Is every bout with infertility, every incurable cancer, every foreclosure, every job loss a direct intervention of God, a clear-cut sign, the perfect outcome? I'll give you an honest answer. *I don't know.* But I don't think so.

Maybe your pain is something he specifically brought into your life because it's part of a greater plan. But maybe it's simply one of the many tragic effects of a world broken by sin. Maybe it was just an accident. God does not reveal the reason behind every heartache. But we can know this: *God will never waste a hurt.* Whatever the cause of your pain, he will work through it to bring new life. There's always a *yes* after every *no*. God says yes to new growth, new frontiers, new blessings that we never see coming.

> There's always a yes after every no. God says yes to new growth, new frontiers, new blessings that we never see coming.

It's a promise embedded deep in the covenant God offered David, so deep some people miss it. Look more closely at his promise. Here's God's *yes* behind this *no*:

> *"The LORD will make you a house. When your days are fulfilled and you lie down with your fathers, I will raise up your offspring after you, who shall come from your body, and I will establish his kingdom. He shall build a house for my*

name, and I will establish the throne of his kingdom forever. I
will be to him a father, and he shall be to me a son."

2 SAMUEL 7:11B–14A ESV

Hmmm. So a descendant of David will have a kingdom that lasts forever. God will be like a father to him, and he will be like a son of God.

These are some of the most important verses in the Bible, in both Jewish and Christian tradition. They are usually referred to as "the Davidic Covenant," the first major covenant (or agreement) between God and humans since Moses.

How did God fulfill this promise? Did David's kingdom last forever? Under his grandson the kingdom fractured in a civil war. David's descendants ruled over the southern kingdom of Judah for a while longer, but the dynasty eventually ended. Nation after nation added to his people's woes.

Yet the people of Israel remembered the prophecy. It became to the Bible what the central melody is to a symphony, echoing and expanding and returning all through Scripture. *A Son of David will reign forever.* This idea is repeated again and again— sometimes with intriguing extra details.

For to us a child is born, to us a son is given, and the
government will be on his shoulders. And he will be called
Wonderful Counselor, Mighty God, Everlasting Father,
Prince of Peace. Of the greatness of his government and
peace there will be no end. He will reign on David's throne
and over his kingdom... from that time on and forever.

ISAIAH 9:6,7 NIV

Out of the stump of David's family will grow a shoot—yes, a new Branch bearing fruit from the old root.

ISAIAH 11:1 NLT

"The days are coming," declares the LORD, "when I will raise up for David a righteous Branch, a King who will reign wisely and do what is right and just in the land. In his days Judah will be saved and Israel will live in safety. This is the name by which he will be called: The LORD Our Righteous Savior."

JEREMIAH 23:5,6 NIV

As Sandra Richter puts it:

As the years go by and the storm clouds continue to gather on the horizon, the same question begins to form itself in the heart of every faithful Israelite: "Is there a son of David out there somewhere who can clean up the mess we've made, stand against our enemies, and speak up for the voiceless?" But the sons of David continue to disappoint.[6]

By the time Jesus was born a thousand years after David, anticipation of the Messiah (literally, "The Anointed One") was at a fever pitch. The gospels of Matthew and Luke both trace Jesus' lineage back to David. As Jesus grew up and began to teach that the kingdom of God was near, many believed this descendant of David would fulfill their dreams for a political restoration of David's empire.

But God said no.

He said *no* to their dreams of political liberation, *no* to their hopes for a political Messiah.

Yet there was a *yes* behind that *no*. Jesus fought a much more powerful enemy, removed a much greater oppression, and brought a much larger kingdom.

David reigned a few decades, but the Son of David is on the throne forever.

David enlarged Jerusalem, but Jesus brings a New Jerusalem.

David wanted to *build* the Temple, but Christ came to *replace* the Temple—with himself.

David fought to free his people from enemy armies, but Jesus fought to free us from our universal enemy: sin.

And just as God extended a covenant to David, he now extends the new covenant to you and me.

> *After supper Jesus took another cup of wine and said, "This cup is the new covenant between God and his people—an agreement confirmed with my blood, which is poured out as a sacrifice for you."*
>
> LUKE 22:20 NLT

He offers to bring you into his house... forever. It's the ultimate yes overriding every no.

Now you simply have to make David's choice: *Will you choose to be blessed with God's blessing—the blessing of the New Covenant?*

This story of how David responds to God's *no* is striking a chord deep in me. We emerge from the underground chambers at the City of David and I blink in the surprising sunlight. I ask Danny for a few minutes to myself.

As I stand outside, watching the beautiful shafts of light pierce the dispersing storm clouds, it's easy to imagine David praying here, his heart overflowing with adoration and wonder. In prayer I paraphrase his words, spoken in his palace somewhere on this very hill.

Sovereign Lord,
Who am I, that you should choose me to bless me?
What more can I say? You know what I am really like!
Because of your kind heart you have been so good to me.
You are God. I am not.

Though you seem to be saying no to this dream
I will remember:
How you did awesome things for your people
How you have done great things for me
How you have promised good things for me
Because of your new covenant
Sealed forever by the Son of David, Jesus Christ.

And to think that it pleases you to bless me!
Lord...
With your blessing, I will choose to be blessed.

Something starts changing inside of me. Slowly. But definitely. Perhaps my strange ennui headed into this trip came because my own dreams, my ambitions, haven't all turned out as I'd hoped and prayed. But that's okay.

With your blessing, Lord, I will choose to be blessed.

DIGGING DEEPER

TEMPLE ZERO

Mysteries keep emerging from the ground beneath the City of David. In 2010 archaeologist Eli Shukron found four small rooms that had been hidden behind a false wall for over 3,000 years. The rooms had been deliberately filled with sandy soil and walled off. After his team carefully removed the fill dirt, they found several clues that they interpreted as evidence these rooms had once been used for sacrificial purposes: remnants of an altar, a sacred stone monument known as a matzevah, loops chiseled into the rock (probably to tie animals before they were sacrificed), small channels in the bedrock likely used to drain away blood, and large quantities of animal bones found in a pit right below the rooms.

Shukron calls these rooms "Temple Zero," the earliest indication of a temple in Jerusalem. The construction is extremely ancient, the rock walls showing signs of being chiseled not with metal implements but with stone tools. Shukron believes the space may date back to the era of Melchizedek, the high priest of God who met with Abraham here centuries before David.[7]

But... why were these rooms deliberately hidden? At one point in the distant past, they had been cleared of all their sacred temple implements and sealed up, never to be used again. Could they have been decommissioned when David brought the Ark of the Covenant to Jerusalem? The mystery continues.

✳

SIX

FINDING GRACE WHEN YOU FALL

2 SAMUEL 11,12

I
DANGER: FALLING KING

Chasing David means following him when he falls. So today I'm back at the City of David, looking down from the rooftop above his former palace. It was somewhere near this spot that he took a moral tumble—and nearly took down an entire empire.

I once read a book by an insurance actuary who pointed out how the spots we tend to associate with danger are actually quite secure. Just about the safest place in the world is the cabin of a commercial airplane 30,000 feet in the air. One of the most dangerous? Your own home. For example, to an insurance agent, your kitchen's a minefield. Spilled water leads to slips. Scalding water causes burns. Sharp pointy objects lurk in every drawer, just waiting to poke and puncture.

But the most lethal spot in your house? The roof. Roofing is the fourth most dangerous job in the U.S., yet homeowners scramble up all the time to grab errant Frisbees or empty clogged gutters. You'd never suit up as a soldier or firefighter or police officer without training, yet roofing is statistically more dangerous than any of those professions (only loggers, fishers, and test pilots have riskier careers).[1]

David is about to discover the risks of his roof.

We've seen David fight on battlefields, hide in caves, flee to an oasis—yet the most perilous place will turn out to be his palace. Because after all his military victories, the one person David can't consistently conquer... is himself.

THE ROOFTOP, DAVID'S HOUSE

> *In the spring of the year, when kings normally go out to war, David sent Joab and the Israelite army to fight the Ammonites... David, however, stayed behind in Jerusalem. Late one afternoon, after his midday rest, David got out of bed and was walking on the roof of the palace.*
>
> 2 SAMUEL 11:1,2 NLT

Jerusalem in the springtime has what I'd call perfect weather, much milder than the surrounding desert because of its altitude—about 4,000 feet above the Dead Sea. The average daytime high temperature in Jerusalem in the spring is 71 degrees (about 21 Celsius) and it gets down to about 54 at night (around 12 Celsius). As this springtime story starts, David's had his nap, he's relaxed, the weather's fine, and it's time to go out on the deck and enjoy the garden view.

> *As he looked out over the city, he noticed a woman of unusual beauty taking a bath.*
>
> **2 SAMUEL 11:2 NLT**

When I was younger I imagined David as a lecher lurking behind a chimney or peering out through half-drawn curtains. But as I stand in the spot that archaeologist Eilat Mazar believes likely to have been David's palace, the setting for this story becomes so much clearer.

II
SETTING FOR A SCANDAL

Let me build the stage set for this drama in your mind. As we've explored already, the palace of the City of David was built on a thin ridge south of the Temple Mount. The slope falls off dramatically on both sides of the ridge. On the eastern slope there's an especially steep decline from the hilltop to the narrow Kidron Valley over one hundred feet below.

To stabilize and protect the steep hillside, the ancient inhabitants of Jerusalem reinforced it with masonry. The eastern slope was covered with what archaeologists call the "Stepped Stone Structure," a series of terraces like a huge retaining wall.

It was built so solidly that a 60-foot section of this massive structure survives to this day.

Archaeologists have found traces of an elaborate irrigation system along some of the terraces leading into the ravine. They believe that in David's era the Gihon Spring was partially diverted into these channels, watering a lavish hillside garden and a park in the valley. So the view facing east from the palace would have been astonishing—a cascade of terraced gardens leading to a lush oasis in the ravine, and as the land rises again on the other side of the valley, the gentle green of an olive orchard. David must have enjoyed the sight often, especially in late afternoon when the sunset behind him illuminated the gardens with "magic hour" golden hues. And he would have seen rooftops. Because every other home in the city was below his.

DIGGING DEEPER

AHIEL'S HOUSE

In the early 1980s, professor Yigal Shilo made a fascinating discovery at the City of David site—the remains of lavish houses built into the terrace known as the Stepped Stone Structure. One of the homes was remarkably well preserved. It's a two-story structure with both floors still partially intact. Scholars even know who the last inhabitant was, because they've found his name on objects inside: Ahiel. He must have been wealthy, because his house even had an interior restroom—with an easily recognizable ancient stone toilet seat!

Ahiel's home apparently had a flat roof that functioned as a balcony for taking in the view. And, probably, for bathing on warm spring evenings.

✳

When I stood on the possible site of David's former palace, it was easy to see how he could have accidentally spotted a woman bathing on a rooftop just below him. His mistake? He kept looking. Then he went further. He imagined the possibilities. Then he went even further. He began making plans.

> *He sent someone to find out who she was, and he was told, "She is Bathsheba, the daughter of Eliam and the wife of Uriah the Hittite."*
>
> 2 SAMUEL 11:3 NLT

Very intriguing foreshadowing in this little verse. She is the daughter of Eliam, named in 2 Samuel 23:34 as one of David's 37 best soldiers, his "mighty men." These were the men who had lived with David all the way back to the Cave of Adullam days, his closest companions, having fought with him through all the ups and downs since then.

But that's not all. Bathsheba is also the wife of Uriah, named in 2 Samuel 23:39 as *another* of the mighty men. So she's *married* to one of David's closest allies and the *daughter* of another.

And there's even more. 2 Samuel 23:34 says her father Eliam was the son of Ahithophel of Giloh, apparently the same person identified in 2 Samuel 15:12 as David's court advisor. So Bathsheba was the *wife* of one of David's closest brothers-in-arms, and the *daughter* of another, and the *granddaughter* of another. David is about to make long-lasting enemies within his own circle of confidantes.

> *Then David sent messengers to get her, and when she came to the palace, he slept with her. Later, when Bathsheba*

discovered that she was pregnant, she sent David a message, saying, "I am pregnant."

2 SAMUEL 11:4,5 NLT

The Bible holds nothing back in this story. In fact it's so blunt that pastors, rabbis, and artists through the centuries have invented all sorts of improbable rationalizations to excuse David's lustful behavior.

When nervous medieval artists painted this scene they showed David glancing sideways at a fully clothed Bathsheba, demurely washing her bare feet while otherwise fully clothed. Apparently this modest moment was all that led to David's affair. Must have been some nice feet.

A rabbinical tradition preserved in the Talmud insists that Bathsheba bathed behind a wicker screen meant to preserve her modesty, but Satan mischievously assumed the form of a bird and landed on the screen. David then shot an arrow at the bird—completely unaware there was a bare-naked lady back there—and when the arrow missed the bird and knocked down the screen, he was shocked—Shocked!—to see her there.[2] So really, everything that followed was Satan's fault.

These elaborate rationalizations remind me of the excuses we all sometimes try to escape guilt: *She made me, it's not as bad as it sounds, the devil made me do it.* But the Bible doesn't give David an inch of rationalization room. It shows him as a voyeur who brazenly indulged his sexual appetites despite the warnings. He's guilty. Period.

And its picture of him gets far worse than that. When David finds out Bathsheba is pregnant, he is cold and selfish, only concerned about covering up, only thinking about his reputation. He quickly plots a coverup.

Plan One: Call Bathsheba's husband, Uriah, back from the war, and get him to sleep with his wife. Then David could plausibly deny he was the father of the child. Uriah refuses because, he says, "The Ark of God and the army are living in tents," and so in symbolic solidarity with his men he sleeps outside the palace gate instead of in his own house.

Plan Two: Get Uriah drunk. Then tell him to go home and go to bed with Bathsheba. But even drunk, Uriah's moral compass works better than David's. It tells him, don't bed down in luxury when your men are fighting a war.

Plan Three: Put Uriah in the front lines and then have the army withdraw, so maybe he'll die in battle. And that's exactly what happens. David even has Uriah carry the sealed order for his own fatal reassignment to the commander. When David hears that Uriah has indeed been killed, his response is horribly casual and cold-blooded, essentially, "Oh well, the sword devours one of ours today, one of theirs tomorrow! Carry on, men!"

He thinks he has gotten away with everything.

Then Nathan the prophet, who I picture as an ancient version of the old TV detective Columbo (look him up on YouTube if don't know what I'm talking about because it makes this story funnier) says, "Uh, king, I got a situation I need your amazing wisdom for... I, I don't know what to do about this. It's crazy."

And Nathan tells a story. My paraphrase (picture Peter Falk mumbling): "King David, it's like this. You're gonna think this is nuts, I don't know why I'm even botherin' you with this ("Go on, Nathan," David urges). Okay... I know this guy who had one cute little lamb. You're not gonna believe this, but he kept it as a pet! He and his kids, they loved that thing, they trained it, they fed it at their table, it would go to sleep in their arms, you should have seen it. So cute. I mean it was adorable.

"But here's the thing, O most wise king. There's this rich character down the road who raises livestock commercially. Has hundreds of sheep. Hundreds! Then the other day, well, weirdest thing happens. Some wealthy guests come into town to stay with him, he wants to have a nice barbecue, and he sends some of his guys to sneak in and steal his neighbor's pet lamb—and butchers the poor man's pet to feed to his guests!"

David burns with anger and says, "That man should die! And then he should pay for that lamb four times over. Well, let's make him pay first—and *then* he should die."

Nathan stops. Points his finger at David. Pauses for effect. And says, *"You are that man!"*

Immediately David realizes—*I'm so busted.*

III
PRELUDE TO A FALL

Before we see what happened next, let's pause. How did David get to the point where he sinned like this? I see four warning signs in David's story:

- *Unaccountable privacy*

  David, however, stayed behind in Jerusalem.

  2 SAMUEL 11:1

In that one little sentence are the seeds of his destruction. Maybe David even planned it this way. He's all alone in the city. His men are gone. No accountability, no supervision, seemingly no chance he'll ever be caught. When we humans are behind closed doors, with no one watching, sometimes our worst tendencies emerge.

- *Unresolved tension*

Back in 2 Samuel 6, David's first wife Michal "despised him in her heart" when she saw him dancing in worship as the Ark is being brought into the city. We never read about that conflict being resolved. In fact verse 23, which observes that Michal bore David no children, seems to imply that their sexual relationship went into permafrost.

- *Unwise compromise*

David gets up on his roof and looks—and keeps looking. The fact is, you're also going to see things in life that will lure you. So will you look on—or look away? This great king becomes a voyeur.

- *Unheeded warnings*

I believe that in his answer to David's question about the identity of the bathing beauty, the unnamed servant tried to warn him. He fires a warning shot across the bow concisely and discretely, essentially saying: "This is Bathsheba... married to one of your mighty men, and the daughter of another. Do not cross these people." But David doesn't listen.

And of course all this begs the question for you and me: How do you see these same warning signals as part of *your* life right now? They are probably there now, to some degree or another. Do what you can to address them. Don't wait for the fall.

THE VIRTUAL ROOFTOP, YOUR HOUSE

These warnings are more relevant than ever. The Internet has made it easy for any of us to be a *virtual* rooftop voyeur. And that rooftop is a very dangerous place to be. In my years as a pastor, every man I've known who had an affair has told me it started with pornography. Looking it over leads to living it out.

Consider this: Beverage companies pay millions for 30-second commercials during events like the Super Bowl because they know that, when seen in tiny increments over time, even short commercials influence consumer choices. When I see someone on TV drinking an ice-cold Coke, sometimes I want an ice-cold Coke too, even though I don't even like Coke! Or anything ice-cold!

So how is it that we as a culture understand the power of advertising and yet don't understand the impact of sexually explicit videos? They are commercials for affairs. And affairs undermine families, the basic building block of a stable society. Look at these ads for affairs long enough and they *will* impact your behavior, your "consumer choices." So don't stand on the rooftop gazing. Look away.

Russell Brand, an actor known for his hard-partying past, became an unexpected crusader against porn when he posted a six-minute video on his YouTube channel about the havoc pornography has created in his own life, and the growing research detailing porn's adverse effects. Within weeks his video had gone viral, garnering millions of views (and showing that many others want help quitting porn too).

I find his passion on this issue compelling precisely because he does *not* come from a religious point of view. He isn't urging people to stop because porn is on someone's list of sins. He's against it because ultimately he found it to be destructive and enslaving. As Brand says, while sexually explicit material has always been around, there are now "icebergs of filth floating through every house on WiFi," saturating willing minds with erotica at levels human society has never experienced, with unforeseeable consequences. He quotes research from *The Journal of Adolescent Health* suggesting unrestrained access to porn adversely impacts the sexual and relational development of young people for years. He says that's exactly what happened to him.

Of course our culture seems to promote destructive sexual behavior in other ways too. A 2019 episode of the NPR podcast *Hidden Brain* about the "hookup culture" on college campuses (the expectation of casual sex between strangers) featured an interview with Lisa Wade, a sociologist at Occidental College and the author of *American Hookup: The New Culture of Sex on Campus*. In her observation, what at first seems fun and harmless can quickly turn depressing and destructive. She found that women in particular begin with hopes that hookups will be liberating, but often end up feeling used and discarded. "Hookup culture," she said, "demands carelessness, rewards callousness, and punishes kindness... the culture is very toxic."[3]

Again, I found her interview intriguing because she does not approach this topic as a Christian; her conclusions are entirely based on academic research. And of course I don't quote her in order to judge those college students, who God infinitely and unconditionally loves, but to demonstrate that there are informed people in our current culture even outside church circles sounding similar warnings about casual sex.

WHAT FANTASIES NEVER SHOW

Brand says a wise man once told him, "The worst thing about porn isn't what it shows. It's what it *doesn't* show." It doesn't show any *consequences*. Yet eventually the emotional, physical, and spiritual consequences to promiscuity can be grave. As Brand says he discovered. And as David is about to learn.

Much of the rest of David's narrative is about the consequences of this affair—and his polygamous lifestyle in general. This wasn't the first time David indulged his sex drive in ways that would raise eyebrows even today; he apparently collected bed partners like a hobby. The Bible identifies at least nine different wives—and that doesn't include his concubines, who numbered at least ten (2 Samuel 15:16). So that's nineteen women in his harem, not to mention any other possible Bathsheba-like one night stands. And why not? Nothing bad ever seemed to happen to him because of his habits. Not for years anyway.

That's a warning for you and me too. Whether in the area of sexual compromise or uncontrolled anger or spending or eating or drinking or substance abuse or anything else, we can make poor decisions in the same direction for a long time and assume that, because no negative consequences have yet happened, they never will. But David's lack of restraint has been leading him toward this single moment, the decision that finally tips the scales. You can pile up twigs on the proverbial camel's back for a long time, but one day, one straw will be one too many.

The ripple effects of David's escapades with Bathsheba and others will grow into a tidal wave that blows apart David's family and kingdom and forces him to flee his own palace. The various women who'd been in his bed gave birth to at least 23 children (that we know of) who would grow up to contend with each other, sometimes violently.

THE EROTIC RISKS OF LEADERSHIP

It's interesting that this affair happens when David is no longer on the run but in charge, building a kingdom. The Bible describes how Israel's territory expanded rapidly during this period, from about 6,000 to 60,000 square miles. To guard all that land David was engaged in constructing fortresses and training soldiers and opening trade routes. Lots of administrative headaches, tons of decisions to make. It all fits with what researchers now know about human vulnerability to temptation. It's when our minds are taxed with decisions that we are weakest.

> It's when our minds are taxed with decisions that we are weakest.

Ever wonder why well-known politicians and CEOs—people with so much to lose—engage in risky sexual behavior? In the Istanbul airport on the flight home I ran across a book by Rolf Dobelli, *The Art of Thinking Clearly*. He quotes research showing that people tasked with making lots of high-level decisions, like executives and administrators (and, I'll add, parents, physicians, pastors and many others who find themselves making decisions constantly), tend to be more susceptible to erotic temptation. Why? He has an interesting theory. Their willpower is sapped. Their brains are tired.[4]

Scientists call it *decision fatigue*. Making executive decisions is exhausting. It requires willpower, and willpower is like a battery. If you've been using it a lot, it gets weak and needs to be recharged. So, he says, make sure you eat, sleep, exercise, and vacation regularly. Take rest very seriously. That's how you recharge your willpower. If you're constantly working and thinking about work, you may be setting yourself up for a willpower crisis.

There's an interesting hint that the narrator of the Book of Samuel sees David in exactly this light, as a weary administrator who's grown used to pushing people around and having orders obeyed: the subtle repetition of the word *send*. "David *sent* Joab... David *sent* someone to inquire about her... David *sent* messengers to get her... David *sent* word to Joab... *Send me* Uriah..." The same David who had always been busily engaged in activity is now ensconced on his throne, dispatching orders according to his whims. As Eugene Peterson points out, "Verb by verb, we watch David remove himself... to a position outside and above others, giving orders, exercising power."[5]

> Willpower is like a battery. If you've been using it a lot, it gets weak and needs to be recharged.

Whether you're vulnerable due to an overtaxed brain or simply because of unregulated fantasies, as always, moral or immoral action starts in the mind. Thoughts breed actions, actions breed habits, habits breed destinies. So what are you pondering as you gaze from your rooftop? You tend to find whatever you're looking for.

IV
ROOFTOP VIEW, OLD CITY, JERUSALEM

Later in the day I clamber up a steep iron staircase to a fantastic vista above the Old City of Jerusalem. Danny showed me the way here a few days ago and I've returned several times since. It's a relatively quiet spot, literally perched on the tops of houses and shops, far removed from the din of the marketplace below. From here I can see across the surreal field of eaves, domes, gables, TV antennas, and chimneys that comprise the canopy of Jerusalem—like London chimney sweep territory in *Mary Poppins*, only instead of the dome of St. Paul's in the distance I see the golden Dome of the Rock.

Here on the roof I try to resolve the tension David's rooftop fall has created inside me. Because it has raised an obvious question: could part of my melancholy be related to buried guilt?

I haven't sinned precisely the same way David did, but I am very aware of the fact that I have been extremely far from perfect—in all areas of my life, including my relationships, my sexual thoughts, and my self-control. In fact lately most of my self-talk seems to be, *You're so stupid; how could you have done that?* as I wince and shudder over past missteps. Even when I get a compliment, I brush it aside with the thought: *I am so not worthy to be seen the way this person sees me.* In my recent doldrums, even comments and cards meant to encourage seem instead to have driven the depression deeper, because of the thought: *I'm a fake, a forgery. A failure.*

I need some hope. I reach into my backpack, take out that travel-worn Bible, and turn to David's heartfelt prayer of confession, Psalm 51.

✧   ✧   ✧

When David realizes all has been discovered, he—at last—does something right. He doesn't cover up, he doesn't rationalize, he doesn't delay—he just confesses. Confesses it all. He goes straight to God in prayer and writes the famous Psalm 51 to express his desperation and contrition.

This psalm is such a rich piece of art, an honest portrait of a soul in crisis. It's a great one to bookmark and read often.

See, if all this talk about sinful compromise is making you feel depressed and guilty because of your own less-than-flawless past, remember: David's story isn't just about his *fall*. It's also about his *recovery*.

> Everyone falls. Many Christians simply do not know how to recover.

This is so important. Because everyone falls, in some way. But in my observation, many Christians simply don't know how to recover. They often slink from church and slip from faith because they're embarrassed. They don't know how to come back to God after they come back to their senses.

David's words here offer a model for me. I need hope. I find it as I begin to read:

> Have mercy on me, O God,
>   because of your unfailing love.
> Because of your great compassion,
>   blot out the stain of my sins.

PSALM 51:1 NLT

Instantly a word jumps out at me. Right there in verse one.

Unfailing. No matter how hard I try, that word will never apply to me. I will never be unfailing. Not in anything. Not ever.

But God is. His love is unfailing. His promise is unfailing. His strength is unfailing. His creativity is unfailing. His calling is unfailing. His purpose is unfailing. His power to restore and resurrect is unfailing. His offer to forgive and set free is unfailing.

I breathe a sigh of relief—mixed still with a little disbelief. *Why do I keep forgetting this?* The Christian life is *not about me.* It's not about my failures. Or my successes. It's about the unfailing God.

It's true for you too. Remember, the Bible says just as God chose David, he chose you. And he will never *unchoose* you. He has a future for you. God does not want you to be chained to past mistakes and regrets. In fact, He made an astounding sacrifice on a cross here in Jerusalem precisely to slice those chains off.

I notice something else in that verse. David does not say, "God forgive me because I am not as bad as that other guy; God, if you forgive me then I'll never do it again; God, if you forgive me I'll give all my money to charity." There's no bargaining. No promising. No comparing.

> God does not want you to be chained to past mistakes and regrets.

He simply says, in essence, "God, have grace, *because you are a gracious God.*" Forgiveness is contingent on the character of God, not the behavior of David.

Then some other verses grab my attention:

Purify me from my sins;
wash me, and I will be whiter than snow...
Create in me a clean heart...

PSALM 51:7,10A NLT

Those verbs are not about penance he is promising. They're about action he is requesting. *Purify me. Wash me. Create in me.* Again, he knows there is nothing he can do to purify *himself. God* must do it.

Renew a loyal spirit within me.

PSALM 51:10B NLT

David doesn't just want technical forgiveness so he can go out and do it again. He wants to stop. He wants to change. And he realizes it is a heart issue.

Restore to me the joy of your salvation, and make me
willing to obey you.

PSALM 51:12 NLT

I love the honesty there. David is admitting, "I am truly sorry but... a large part of me actually still does not *want* to obey. Make me *willing* to obey you, help me *want* to do what's right." This verse links that willingness to joy. David rightly perceives that the joy we find in the Lord is key to making us want to follow him. If all I feel when I think of God is condemnation, then I am not going to want to be near Him. But if I find *joy* there, I will want to follow Him.

And here's the most stunning verse:

You do not desire a sacrifice, or I would offer one. You do not want a burnt offering. The sacrifice you desire is a broken spirit. You will not reject a broken and repentant heart, O God.

PSALM 51:16,17 NLT

David sees that the blood of animal sacrifices does not take away sin. In fact, he says he *won't* do religious rituals just to symbolically atone for what he has done. Why not?

I think he understands that this can turn into a destructive pattern. You commit the sin, then do the religious ritual and feel you're clean, then you sin again, do the ritual again, sin, ritual, sin, ritual. It's impersonal, like paying the fine for illegal parking. You don't like the cost, but maybe it was worth it for you.

If all I feel when I think of God is condemnation, then I am not going to want to be near Him. But if I find *joy* there, I will want to follow Him.

David understands that it is *always* personal. My sin is an offense to God, the same God who loves me and has blessed me so much. So God's desire is not for impersonal penance. It's for a restoration of that intimate relationship with him.

This is the key to recovering from a fall: not just doing *religion*, but returning to a vital *relationship* with God. Of course this anticipates Christianity by a thousand years. David's words foreshadow the day, very close to the spot where he prayed this prayer, when Jesus would stop all those sacrifices with one last great sacrifice—of himself. Now God truly does not desire ritual sacrifice from anyone anymore—ever. What he wants are hearts softened and yielded to him.

V

THE GIFT OF REPENTANCE

Have you crossed any of the lines that David crossed—or some other lines you know you shouldn't have—and you're now living in shame and guilt?

I strongly suggest taking out your own Bible and reading Psalm 51. Let David's words sink in deep. You failed. But God is *unfailing*.

And then... *Repent*.

People can perceive the word "repent" as negative, used only by angry street corner prophets, but I'm discovering it's a great word. Repentance is God's gift. The offer to repent means God doesn't just throw you out with each misstep. Repentance means you can move *forward* again—and stop looking backwards.

> Repentance is God's gift.

Repentance means God is giving you a chance to turn around, to turn from your self-centered, self-destructive behavior—and all the shame that comes with it—and face Him. That idea might scare you. Maybe you're afraid of what you'll see: a scowling face, a frown, a snarl. But when you turn toward God again you'll see his eyes of wisdom, power, and love. And you'll hear his voice.

It whispers, *beloved*.

YOU'RE SURROUNDED

Perhaps you're so deep in your self-destructive habit that you worry you can't stop. You say, *I have no resolve.* Can you at least pray, *God, create a willing spirit within me,* as David did? I guarantee you that even now, God is already providing answers to that prayer.

As God provided Nathan for David, God is already providing you with people and support groups and books and web sites and other resources to help you get back on track. They are there waiting for you right now at your church, in your community, in online forums, in bookstores, among your friends. You are literally surrounded by help.

Start plugging into those resources today. Get into a group at your church. Confide in a trusted friend. Order a book about recovery. Look up recovery web sites. If it's substance abuse you're dealing with, try www.nacr.org for a start. If sexual addiction is your struggle, try the book *Secrets: A True Story of Addiction, Infidelity, and Second Chances* by Jonathan Daugherty.

Do something. Start today. Be positive and proactive. Stop thinking that if you only feel guilty enough, you'll change. Guilt is not enough. Get help. And keep getting help.

What if you weren't the cheater—you were the cheated? When you discovered your loved one's unfaithfulness, you felt like you were punched in the gut. You wandered in disbelief, alternating between wanting to hide it all and wanting to shout out your mate's indiscretion to the world. Maybe you can still hardly believe it. I am so sorry for your hurt. And I want you to know there's hope and there's help.

> Stop thinking that if you only feel guilty enough, you'll change.

You're surrounded too. The bad news is, your experience is more common than you probably realize. The good news is, you are consequently living in an age of plentiful resources for marriages in crisis. Books and web sites and counselors and retreats abound, all around you. Get help now. One suggestion: Try starting with affairecovery.com.

When you seek help, you're not doing it for your unfaithful spouse. You're doing it for yourself. Because bitterness can fester like an infection for years until it destroys your joy in ways even worse than the initial injury.

DELAYED CONSEQUENCES

I believe bitterness about the Bathsheba affair was just beneath the worst betrayal David would ever experience. When David's son Absalom hatches a conspiracy against his father years later, he is joined by some of David's own mighty men—and worst of all, Absalom's chief advisor, the one whispering strategy in his ear, is none other than Ahithophel, Bathsheba's grandfather!

I think this explains the bizarre advice given by Ahithophel after Absalom captures David's palace (2 Samuel 16:20,21). Ahithophel tells him that first, before he does anything else, it is very important for Absalom to take all ten of David's concubines to the roof of the palace (the very place David leered at Bathsheba) and sleep with them in public.

It's not hard to imagine that Ahithophel feels he's somehow paying David back for what he did to his granddaughter. He is going to make David feel Uriah's pain, the pain of a jilted husband ten times over. But in his cruelty to these women, his bitterness has made him into the very misogynistic monster he thought he saw in David.

Keeping silent about your transgression—or your injury from someone else's transgression—only drives that hurt deeper. It can turn you into a bitter monster.

That's why, in another psalm written after he repents, David writes:

When I kept silent,
my bones wasted away through
my groaning all day long.
For day and night your hand was heavy on me
my strength was sapped as in the heat of summer.
Then I acknowledged my sin to you
and did not cover up my iniquity.
I said, "I will confess my transgressions to the LORD."
And you forgave the guilt of my sin.

PSALM 32:3–5 NIV

Whether you're the cheated or the cheater, break the silence. Get help.

Though there are many twists to the plot, eventually David is restored to effective leadership—and to lasting ministry through psalms composed about this fall and rise. Bathsheba has great impact too; she marries David, and, though her first child with David would die tragically shortly after birth, their son Solomon will become the wisest king in Israel's history. And many generations later, a direct descendant of David and Bathsheba would change world history. His name was Jesus.

The sun sets behind me, making the golden Dome of the Rock shine even more brilliantly as I take out my pocket journal and quickly jot down three principles for restoration I see here in Psalm 51:

1. Admit your guilt. Do not bargain, minimize, or excuse it. Take complete ownership, without blaming.

2. Focus on God's unfailing love, not your failure. Realize God has mercy on you because he is merciful, not because you deserve it. When you understand this, then you are set free to make amends in an unburdened, honest way. You won't make amends to earn someone's approval or win their forgiveness; you already have the forgiveness of God, so you can simply do the right thing because it's the right thing to do.

3. Find ways to restore spiritual joy, rather than wallowing in guilt. It's your joy in God's presence that will empower you and draw you closer to God. And the closer you are to God, the more you'll want to keep walking with him.

Maybe you're not in a place right now where you specifically need to return to God after sexual sin, as David was. But you still somehow feel far from him, like your spiritual burners are set on low. You feel like a failure. You need a power boost. That's exactly how I felt on that rooftop.

One line from Psalm 51 kept echoing in my head. I closed my eyes and made David's prayer my own, from a very deep place in my soul.

Restore to me the joy of your salvation.

When you pray that prayer, then you really are on the trail of King David. As he did for David, God can lift you into his arms after those rooftop falls, and carry you back up the royal hill, into the palace, all the way to the banquet table, where the taste of grace is even sweeter because you hunger for it so deeply—and know you need it so desperately.

But even as David returns to faith and obedience, there is an enemy lurking in the palace halls with secret schemes of his own.

DIGGING DEEPER

THAT SEALS IT

Other exciting discoveries near the City of David help confirm this was the administrative center of ancient Jerusalem. The most conclusive finds contain the actual names of people in the Bible.

Clay seals, or *bullae*, were found with the names "Jehucal the son of Shelemiah" and "Gedaliah, son of Pashhur," named in Jeremiah 38 as members of King Zedekiah's court who opposed Jeremiah the prophet.[6] In March 2019 a seal was discovered with the name "Natan Melech", mentioned in 2 Kings 23:11 as a high-ranking member of the court of King Josiah. Most famously, in 2015 a seal impression was found with the name Hezekiah son of Ahaz. He was a king of Judah, a descendant of David —and an ancestor of Jesus.[7]

Here's why that's so cool. In ancient times, round balls of wet clay were pressed onto the ends of scrolls in order to seal them closed, then whoever had authored the scroll pressed down with their signet ring, like pressing a wax seal on an envelope. Everyone's ring had a unique carving of their name, leaving an impression on the clay which later hardened. Your signet ring was the way you signed documents, pledged collateral on loans, and identified yourself—like your autograph, your credit card, and your ID, all rolled into one. What we have in the *bullae* are essentially the personal signatures of these Bible characters!

SEVEN

FINDING STRENGTH WHEN PEOPLE CAUSE YOU PAIN

2 SAMUEL 15

I
MOUNT OF OLIVES, JERUSALEM

At breakfast in the hotel restaurant I read headlines about the previous afternoon's Temple Mount riot. Sixty violent Palestinian protestors were arrested.

I start to wonder if there will be danger on my walk today; my plan is to go into a Palestinian Arab neighborhood, on the other side of the Mount of Olives. I'd intended to chase down the political tensions in David's Jerusalem by taking the slow walk over the Mount of Olives, just as he did during a family

186 · CHASING DAVID

feud that led to a violent civil war. But similar tensions erupting today in modern Jerusalem may thwart my plans. Of course, there are often tensions like this in the Middle East, particularly between Israeli Jews and Palestinian Arabs. But they are definitely escalating now, just weeks ahead of Israel's presidential election.

I'm immersed in the newspaper story about the violence when I notice the time—and realize with a start that if I intend to carry through with my plans, I need to hit the road right now, before tour buses clog the narrow streets. So after a final gulp of coffee and the exciting discovery that strawberry jam tastes amazing on a Jerusalem bagel, I scramble for the door.

But when the front desk clerk hears I'm headed for a Palestinian neighborhood, she stops me and insists on arranging for a taxi driven by an Arab. She picks up the phone and calls a guy she knows.

Her alarmed reaction amid all this political unease has me slightly worried about what I'll encounter with this driver. Where does he stand in all this tension? Will he see me, an American, as part of the problem? What about the language barrier?

I wait at the hotel curb. A black Renault taxi pulls up. The Arab driver looks me over and beckons me toward the car. Before I'm seated, he stops me. "Where you from?" he demands. I wonder, *Is this like a passenger screening?* I nervously tell him, "California—The Bay Area."

He smiles and shouts, "I thought so! I lived in San Jose for 16 years, brother! I miss In-N-Out so much!" Turns out my Warriors t-shirt gave me away.

I jump in and we trade Silicon Valley memories as the cab winds through the city streets.

Eventually I feel comfortable enough to ask his opinion about the current political situation. I expect him to try to convince me of his side, but he surprises me. "Yes, there is always drama here, always a new controversy," he answers, "and I pray for a wise solution. But I try also to look at the beauty that never changes. This is the way to stay sane."

We roll through a congested part of town where I notice graffiti and barbed wire and broken glass. He starts pointing out the window. "Look at those flowers along the sidewalk, those birds on the telephone poles, those laughing kids. I tell myself every day, 'Everything good is from God's hands.' He is leaving gifts all around us. We just need to notice." I was worried about tension and I'm getting great advice for life.

"Don't obsess on the news," he tells me. "Look at God, and the gifts he has given all of us. That will make you peaceful enough to love even your enemies."

He drops me off with some final deep words of wisdom—a personal recommendation for a falafel place in Sunnyvale. As he drives away, he yells through the open window, "Remember, everything good is a gift from God's hands!"

I watch his cab leave and it occurs to me that the David I've come to discover would agree with him. I imagine him saying, "Yes, there was always drama, always a new controversy in my life, but in the end, I tried to look at the beauty that never changes. All from God's hands." That's exactly where David eventually goes in the passage I'm about to experience.

❖   ❖   ❖

In a bookshop I had picked up a little paperback by Daniel E. Miller, a long-time resident of Jerusalem, called *When Others Make Life Difficult*. I cracked it open later in my trip and was riveted, reading the whole thing all the way through in one sitting. Miller lists some common ways people exhibit abusive behavior:

- Ridicule
- Slander
- Intimidation
- Criticism
- Rejection
- Mocking
- Blame
- False accusations
- Stalking
- Destruction or theft of property
- Stirring up a mob against you[1]

It occurs to me as I read this: David experienced every single one of those abusive behaviors. And worst of all, many came from his own son.

Of all the threatening people David faced, from Goliath to the Philistine armies to King Saul, none seems to have bewildered and wounded David as much as Absalom.

We live side-by-side with fellow humans. Sometimes that's a blessing. At other times there's friction and tension. Some disagreement is inevitable and normal, but occasionally it escalates. Lines are crossed. People become determined to hurt you and hinder your progress. A relative steals your inheritance. A neighbor is constantly mean. A co-worker gets you fired. Strife spreads like a cancer, mutating into boardroom splits, family feuds, even national wars. It turns into a cycle of retribution. Violence is answered with violence, injustice with injustice. The Middle East has, sadly, seen that cycle many times.

And that's where David finds himself right here, on the Mount of Olives.

After the cab drops me off, I walk through a neighborhood, crest the hill, and see the spectacular postcard view of the Old City of Jerusalem across the Kidron Valley. The ancient walls of lion-colored stone glow golden in the morning sun. There really does seem to be something unique about the quality of light here, something that makes it all seem so special, so sacred.

King David must have seen a similar sight when he walked over this same hill. But he was weeping bitter tears. First he looked back at the city he was leaving, driven out by the civil war his own son started, wondering aloud if he would ever see Jerusalem again. Then he returned over this same road once the war was won—but at a bitter price.

THE DOMINOES FALL

One of the long-term consequences of David's adultery with Bathsheba—and numerous liaisons with other women, both wives and concubines—was the intense conflict this provoked between his children. He had repented of his adultery with Bathsheba, but with his indiscretions, his absentee fathering style, and his unwillingness to hold his own children accountable for their misbehavior, David was setting up dominoes that would topple, one into the other, until they threatened his entire kingdom.

A horrific crime catalyzes the chain reaction. David's daughter Tamar is raped by her own half-brother Amnon. The Bible describes her as a "desolate woman" from then on.

After this tragedy, all the men in Tamar's life let her down. David is furious with Amnon for what he did, but that's it. He's mad. Great. Yet he doesn't pursue any legal recourse.

Meanwhile Tamar's brother Absalom comforts her—and takes care of her for the rest of her life—yet also advises her, "Keep quiet for now, since he's your brother. Don't you worry about it." (2 Samuel 13:20 NLT)

Even though the ancient Mosaic law had penalties for rape, no one prosecutes Amnon for his crime as they should have. Where there should have been justice, there was only anger and embarrassed silence.

BREAKING THE SILENCE

This is not an easy story to read. Tamar's tragedy is upsetting. And it's supposed to be.

The Bible is for mature audiences. It creates moral tension on purpose. There is not always a happy ending to every story. The reader is expected to follow the plot and observe what consequences result from the decisions of each character—in this case, to see how the whole kingdom would suffer for this inaction against Amnon. Years later, what happened to Tamar, and the cover-up and craziness that followed, would come into the open. And the empire would be nearly destroyed in the fallout.

Sadly, Tamar's story is not uncommon. This pattern has continued for 3,000 years as abused women and children are often still told to stay silent. The consequences of ignoring Tamar's pain remind me of what's happening in society today as entire institutions are existentially threatened because of inaction against abusers years ago.

Before we continue the story, I want to say this. You may have been sexually violated yourself, and, as Tamar experienced, people in your life have either ignored it—or sympathized but counseled you to keep it quiet. That is bad advice. Break the silence. Find someone who can help you toward healing, preferably a professional counselor. A crime should be reported to the proper authorities. Keeping quiet about your trauma can only create further conflict. The stress creates fractures in yourself, your relationships, and even entire churches, schools, and other organizations. Like David's own kingdom.

If you haven't experienced this, you probably know someone who has. Tamar is with us still, as your friend, your daughter, your spouse, your co-worker, someone you know who has suffered in a similar way. If you don't like how the biblical Tamar's story ends, that's good. That's one reason this story is in the Bible, so you will be motivated to help write a different ending to the Tamar stories in your life. Stand with your Tamar for healing and justice.

Whatever you do, don't follow Absalom's example. His silent rage against Amnon simmers until, two years later, he exacts a bloody revenge. He gets Amnon drunk at a party—and then murders him and flees the country. Rage is never a good substitute for justice.

Three years go by until David extends Absalom a pardon for his crime of passion and allows him to return. But for the next two years—though Absalom is back living in Jerusalem—David does not speak to him. Not a single word.

Again, he doesn't deal with the moral problem of Absalom's vigilante justice. There's just silence. David's apparent strategy when there are complicated issues in his own family: *Let's not talk about it.*

RUSTY ARMOR

Why do you suppose David continues this unhealthy policy of silence? Robert Fisher's book *The Knight in Rusty Armor* is a parable about a famous knight who often journeys far from home and fights great battles. But the knight is so accustomed to wearing his armor that, when he comes home, he doesn't know how to take it off—in fact, soon he can't. He's worn it so long that it's rusted shut—and even his family can't get close to him anymore.

I think David has a very bad case of rusty armor. He's been so busy battling that he can't slow down to sympathize.

I look around and see people all around me with rusty armor syndrome too. I get touches of it myself. We become so exhausted and calloused by the fights we're in for survival every day at work—or with chores and other duties at home—that we somehow forget to be loving and open to our own families, particularly when they're wounded and need a lot of care.

But hiding inside rusty armor is a lonely way to live. Soon there may be nothing left of our relationships.

Finally David cracks open his visor just an inch. He agrees to see Absalom. But the damage is done. Absalom decides, "I'm sick of my father. They need a new ruler around here. *Me.*"

Already Absalom's been praised as the most handsome man in Israel, flawless from head to toe. Wears his hair long, like a rock star—picture Robert Plant or Peter Frampton in their glory years. Then he starts a campaign of influence that could rival the best politician. For four years he stands in front of the courthouse and tells everyone with a grievance, "You've got a strong case; too bad I'm not in charge around here, I'd support you (implied: *I'd seek justice. Unlike my father*)."

Having won many hearts with this charm offensive, Absalom takes a trip to Hebron, the same city where David was first crowned king. In a deliberate parallel, he anoints himself the new king there. David's advisors report the bad news. "All Israel has joined Absalom in his conspiracy against you!"

And David flees. Instantly, that same day. Eastward, out of the City of David, down into the Kidron Valley, and across to the Mount of Olives:

> *David walked up the road to the Mount of Olives, weeping*
> *as he went.*
>
> 2 SAMUEL 15:30 NLT

David's about 60 years old at this point and once again on the run. He must have been thinking, *When will all this trouble ever end?*

Then something happens that has always intrigued me. A man named Shimei comes running out of a house, cursing David and his men. He even throws rocks at David and the warriors that surround him.

> *"Get out of here, you murderer, you scoundrel!" he*
> *shouted at David. "The LORD is paying you back for all*
> *the bloodshed...At last you will taste some of your own*
> *medicine, for you are a murderer!"*
>
> 2 SAMUEL 16:7,8 NLT

One of David's security detail says, "Let me go over and cut off his head!" But David responds, "No! Who asked your opinion? If the Lord has told him to curse me, who are you to stop him?"

Then David said to Abishai and to all his servants, "My own son is trying to kill me. Doesn't this relative of Saul have even more reason to do so? Leave him alone and let him curse, for the LORD has told him to do it..." So David and his men continued down the road, and Shimei kept pace with them on a nearby hillside, cursing and throwing stones and dirt at David.

2 SAMUEL 16:11,13

By his reaction, David seems to have realized he did deserve at least some of the blame. He is essentially saying, "Hey, maybe I deserve to hear what this character is saying. And if I don't, then perhaps God will bless me for enduring an unfair curse."

When you're in the middle of a conflict, it's good practice to be humble and analyze your own culpability. How have you contributed to the conflict? Can you listen to the things people are saying—even if they are expressing themselves with a little too much horsepower—and hear some kernels of truth?

DIGGING DEEPER

RATS UNEARTH ANCIENT CITY

Thanks in part to burrowing mole rats, another long-lost fortress city associated with King David has emerged.

Mole rats love to tunnel deep into the earth, leaving little piles of excavated dirt on the surface. Archaeologists near Hebron sifted through some of those mounds and found evidence of ancient construction at a site called Tel 'Eton. So they put their spades into the ground—and revealed a 15-acre city that had been lost to history. Professor Avraham Faust, director of the dig, believes it's a crucial milestone in the debate over King David.

The archaeologists reported their finds in 2018 in the Cambridge University journal Radiocarbon, detailing how they were able to carbon-date samples from the site to the 10th century B.C., precisely the time the Bible says David reigned as king.[2] They unearthed complex fortifications and hundreds of artifacts. Construction of this sophistication seems to have emerged in Israelite society suddenly at this time. This is yet more physical evidence that powerful leadership was motivating the tribes living in these hills to rapidly coalesce into a state. As Dr. Faust told reporters, there must have been a sudden "inspiration or cause for the transformation."[3]

"If someone thinks that there was no King David," Dr. Faust argues, "that person should come up with a different name for the highland king in whose time the region was incorporated into the highland kingdom."[4]

✳

11
MOOD SWINGS THAT GET SOMEWHERE

Maybe, like David, you have felt betrayed by someone close to you—a sibling or spouse, relatives or friends, son or daughter, co-worker or boss. Maybe someone has tried to take what belongs to you, like Absalom did in this story. Maybe you're reaping some of the relational consequences you yourself have sown—as was the case with David. Whatever the cause, when others make your life difficult, it's exhausting, demoralizing, and confusing.

> The temptation when others hurt you is to stay in a place of *negative reactive emotion.*

The temptation when others hurt you is either to live in *denial*, or to stay in a place of *negative reactive emotion*, where you respond with constant venom. You spew the poison out toward the people in your life or just toward the universe, constantly rehearsing how badly your life is going.

But David does neither. He doesn't deny his pain. And he learns how to transform his negative reaction emotion into something more constructive.

You can see David's thought process in a song he apparently wrote at this time in his life, Psalm 62. This is a song about what to do when the worst thing you can imagine...happens.

VENTING AND REDIRECTING

Psalm 62 is so dynamic and so real because it shows David going back and forth between wrestling and resting, venting and relenting, hostility and serenity. It's as if, with each couple verses, David's attention swings toward God—*then swings back toward his betrayers.*

I think of God.

I think of my enemies.

God.

Those jerks.

And isn't that the way of our own thoughts? Constantly distracted, forever swinging from peaceful to peeved?

But as you'll see, because David keeps shepherding his own thoughts back toward God, eventually, even when his attention swings back to his enemies, he's able to think of them a little differently.

Watch his mood swings and see how he finds equilibrium:

I wait quietly before God,
   for my victory comes from him.
He alone is my rock and my salvation,
   my fortress where I will never be shaken.

PSALM 62:1,2 NLT

Starts out so relaxed. In a good place. He's got this. He's going to stop thinking negative thoughts and refocus on God, and wait on His good timing.

Then...David's thoughts turn back to the ones who've betrayed him and he gets all worked up again:

So many enemies against one man—
   all of them trying to kill me.
To them I'm just a broken-down wall
   or a tottering fence.

They plan to topple me from my high position.
  They delight in telling lies about me.
They praise me to my face
  but curse me in their hearts.

PSALM 62:3,4 NLT

Those two-timing no-good betrayers! They think I'm old and weak. Even the ones who say nice things to me. I don't trust any of them for one second.

Then he calms himself again and refocuses past the perpetrators:

Let all that I am wait quietly before God,
  for my hope is in him.
He alone is my rock and my salvation,
  my fortress where I will not be shaken.
My victory and honor come from God alone.
  He is my refuge, a rock where no enemy can reach me.
O my people, trust in him at all times.
  Pour out your heart to him,
  for God is our refuge.

PSALM 62:5–8 NLT

Notice how David again describes God with some of his favorite words: *my rock, my fortress, my refuge.*

In his younger days, David literally hid from his enemies in the rocks and caves of the wilderness. This time he crosses the Jordan River and stays in a city of the Ammonites, where a wealthy man invites him into his home and makes him and his men very comfortable. But David is saying, whether I am in a literal cave or in a wealthy ally's home, it's God who is actually my refuge. I can't place my trust fully in people or in fortresses or even in my own morality, because they can all fail me. I place my trust entirely in God as the fortress of my soul.

Okay, great, we are focused on God now. But wait. David thinks again of the bad guys. His thoughts are a little less intense, but still pretty cynical:

> *Common people are as worthless as a puff of wind,*
> *and the powerful are not what they appear to be.*
> *If you weigh them on the scales,*
> *together they are lighter than a breath of air.*
>
> PSALM 62:9 NLT

He's saying, these enemies of mine don't amount to much. And he's advising his listeners, don't be overly impressed by people. Don't think that just because they are "commoners" or just because they are "powerful," that automatically grants them some virtue. David, who's been both a commoner and royalty, has seen these worlds from the inside. He knows: *Lowborn, highborn, people are all the same.* I think it's also a sly criticism of Absalom's charm offensive we saw earlier. David's saying, *these people seem impressive, but really, they're lightweights.*

> I place my trust
> in God as the
> fortress of my soul.

> *Don't make your living by extortion*
> *or put your hope in stealing.*
> *And if your wealth increases,*
> *don't make it the center of your life.*
>
> PSALM 62:10 NLT

Implied here: *Like my enemies do!* But at least here his anger has a lower temperature. It's no longer just about how he's been hurt. It has turned into something a little healthier: a lesson for others. Don't desire wealth and power so much that it rules everything else in your life.

III
GOD'S UNFAILING LOVE AND JUSTICE

Finally David swings away again from a focus on the bad guys back to his favorite two truths about God's nature, qualities he praises God for over and over, throughout his life—God's power and God's love.

> *God has spoken plainly,*
> *and I have heard it many times:*
> *Power, O God, belongs to you;*
> *unfailing love, O Lord, is yours.*
>
> PSALM 62:11 NLT

Power and love. David realizes, *Even if the love of my own son fails, God's love will never fail. And even if I feel powerless, God's power will never falter.*

He reminds himself who God is. And he reminds himself who he is, in relationship with God.

When you can't think of anything else to be thankful for, remember some character qualities of God. They never change. God is all-powerful, all-knowing, omnipresent, eternal, gracious, compassionate.

David ends with one little line that brings God and his enemies into the same picture. It's like his hands folded in prayer begin to get a little white-knuckle-tense again as his thoughts drift back to his betrayers:

> *Surely you repay all people*
> *according to what they have done.*
>
> PSALM 62:12 NLT

That's actually a good place to leave your anger. Be assured that God doesn't overlook wounds caused by injustice. God will right every wrong.

It may not be now. It may wait until the new heaven and the new earth. But somehow, in some way that will satisfy you because you will see that it is absolutely the most righteous thing that He could have done, God will bring justice and healing. God can be completely trusted to do so.

> Even if I feel powerless, God's power will never falter.

I need to mention again that of course David should have brought justice to bear through the available legal means, long before this situation got further out of hand. Trying to pretend Amnon's crime never happened was a very foolish decision with far-reaching consequences.

But David *does* take action at this point. He doesn't just sit in contemplation. He devises strategy. He assigns spies. He has an informer in Absalom's inner court, feeding Absalom disinformation. David organizes a counter-attack. He does what he can to stop this rebellion—but he is able to stay serene because his *hope* in not in his own schemes. His ultimate hope is in God.

The principle? Do what you can when in times of distress. Take constructive, wise steps—but put your ultimate hope in God. That way at least you're moving forward, running to battle, with your confidence firmly in the belief that God will work his purpose even through this, somehow.

THE PROCESS OF FAITH

When life seems unfair, when you feel angry or betrayed, don't just stay focused on the unfairness. And don't deny it either. How do you do that? Follow the pattern of this psalm. Go ahead and complain about the problem. Then focus on God.

The back-and-forth is part of the process. It's a way of really owning your faith, not just parroting what you hear from some teacher. As your attention swings from the trouble to God (the trouble to God, the trouble to God, over and over) your perspective on the problem changes. As you grapple with your feelings, eventually you remember that you're not alone. That you're not dependent on your own strength. That you still have a destiny. That God promises to somehow bring beauty even out of our pain. That's how you get to a place of equilibrium and serenity, instead of staying in a place of reactive negative emotion.

There's even more at stake than your own peace of mind. Daniel Miller writes of walking down a street in Jerusalem, seeing a boy hit another boy. The victim immediately hit back harder. Predictably, the first boy reacted with even more violence. Soon it was an all-out fight. It all happened in seconds, and for Miller it represented in miniature the seemingly endless cycle of violent retribution he saw as a resident of the Middle East: negative reactive emotion keeps escalating the chaos.

Jesus came to break that cycle. When mocked and slandered, he did not retaliate. Even when crucified, he prayed for his tormentors. It was on that day, through that response, with that sacrifice, that he made a way past the cycle of pain.

So consider carefully how you react in the moments after someone provokes you.

My wife experienced this in a memorable way. She is on the advisory board for an organization that provides a children's home, clinic, and school in a developing country known for its growing hostility to Christians. The staff is led by believers who sense a call to this work because of their devotion to Christ. The night before their doors opened for the first time, a group of angry locals vandalized their property, defacing all the signs pointing people to the campus. They slandered and spread rumors about the organization. Angry and worried volunteers asked the director, a woman who had grown up in that country, what they should do. She answered, "Just relax. God will use this."

> When life seems unfair, don't just stay focused on the unfairness.

They held a chapel where they prayed. They didn't deny their anger and fear. They expressed it to God. Then they all focused on their mission. They welcomed the orphan, the poor, the sick. One day a man approached in tears and asked the director, "You helped my wife today when she was in terrible pain, even though we locals tried to scare you away. Why?"

The director replied, "Because we follow Jesus, who told us to bless those who curse us, to bless and not retaliate."

The man wept as he confessed, "I was the man who led those vandals. I vow to you we will repair the damage. You are welcome here." And that man became their biggest fan.

The cycle of negative reactive emotion was broken. The peace of God was spread. And the staff there discovered something that's always true: It's in our response to trials that we become attractive for our faith. Because then others see us living like the Jesus we claim to follow.

THE AFTERMATH

Eventually the rebellion is put down. David is able to return to his kingdom via that Mount of Olives route. But tragically, Absalom himself is killed during the battle.

David's response when he learns of his rebel son's death perplexes his commander-in-chief, Joab. David is deeply shaken and cries out:

> "O my son Absalom! My son, my son Absalom! If only I had died instead of you—O Absalom, my son, my son!"
>
> 2 SAMUEL 18:33 NIV

David's reaction is psychologically true to how parents often respond to their rebellious children. I've seen it many times. Even when deeply wounded, the loving heart of a parent cries out for a wayward child.

MAINTAIN WHAT REMAINS

Although he should have been more sympathetic, Joab's advice to David when he shuts himself up in a dark room, crying over Absalom, has a core of common sense:

"You have made it clear today that the commanders and their men mean nothing to you. Now go out and encourage your men. I swear by the LORD that if you don't go out, not a man will be left with you by nightfall. This will be worse for you than all the calamities that have come on you from your youth till now."

2 SAMUEL 19:7 NIV

Joab wasn't trying to stop David from grieving. He was trying to stop David from doing nothing *but* grieve as events continued to unfold. He was preventing David, in this critical moment, from fatally destroying his remaining healthy relationships.

In our grief over the loss or rebellion of loved ones, we too can sometimes forget to maintain the relationships that are left. It's not easy, but we need to focus not just on our pain but also on the faithfulness and love of those still close to us.

IV
PARALLEL PATHS

As I walk the ancient path on the Mount of Olives, it strikes me that not one but two Bible characters walked this path in tears: David, and his most famous descendant, Jesus. Both were on this very road during greatest crisis of their lives. Both were in tears. Both would be rejected as king. Both would experience the abandonment of all but a few friends.

The major difference?

One walked *away* from the city to *save* his life, and later returned to reestablish his kingdom by putting the pieces of Israel back together.

The other walked *toward* the city to *give* his life, and according to the Bible will one day return to reestablish his kingdom by putting the pieces of the *world* back together.

✦ ✦ ✦

I recall reading that olive trees can live as long as redwoods, up to two thousand years. So it's very likely some of the same olive trees that witnessed David's tears also stood by Jesus when he wept on these slopes a thousand years later.

I see a ton of parallels between those two Mount of Olives moments:

David wept over his rebellious child, Absalom. Jesus wept over his rebellious children, Israel.

David was rejected by those closest to him—including his confidante, Ahithophel. Jesus was rejected by those closest to him—including one of his own disciples, Judas.

Even as many Israelites reject David, 600 Gentile men (from—of all places—Gath, the Philistine city of Goliath!) find him on the Mount of Olives and embrace him. Their commander pledges their allegiance, calling David, "My lord and my king." This foreshadows the Gentile embrace of Jesus as Messiah.

One final parallel between David and Jesus on the Mount of Olives really intrigues me. In sort of an ultimate sign of surrender to God, David tells Zadok the priest:

"If the LORD sees fit, he will bring me back...But if he is through with me, then let Him do as seems best to Him."

2 SAMUEL 15:25,26 NLT

Jesus similarly prayed on the Mount of Olives:
"Father, if you are willing, take this cup of suffering away from me. Nevertheless, your will, not my will be done."

LUKE 22:42 NLT

Basically the same sentiment both times.

"If the LORD sees fit..." *"Father, if you are willing..."*

"But let Him do as seems best to Him..." *"...your will, not my will be done..."*

When you're attacked, when a loved one is attacked, or when there's any kind of unwanted suffering in life, that is the hardest prayer to pray. Yet it's really the ultimate prayer of faith: "God, whatever your will is—*that's* what I want. Now, here's my request, this is what I would *like* you to do. But I want your will above all."

THE REJECTED KING

When David rode back into his city he must have been reminding himself again of God's promise of a stable, eternal dynasty. He surely hoped for peace at last. Instead he found someone else coming through the door with another spear. As you'll see in the next chapter.

But first, fast forward to Jesus.

Less than a week before his crucifixion, Jesus had never been more popular. Throngs of people lined this same road, waving palm branches, welcoming him into Jerusalem. Why? The Palm Sunday crowd was explicitly affirming Jesus as the Messiah, the new anointed one, the next king, the new David.

The crowds that went ahead of Jesus and those that
followed shouted, "Hosanna to the Son of David!"

MATTHEW 21:9 NIV

But Jesus disappointed some and threatened others. So the cheers turned to jeers. All those familiar ways people can make life difficult--ridicule, slander, criticism, rejection, mocking, false accusations, violence, stirring up mobs--reared up again, this time not against David but against the Son of David.

Only unlike David, Jesus did not leave Jerusalem to escape the threats. He deliberately stayed, purposefully giving himself up to the people who would cause him such pain. And his life quickly ended on a Roman cross. There, Jesus paid for the sins of everyone--even those mocking and torturing him in that moment.

> God keeps sending good gifts. They may not be the gifts you expect. But open your eyes a little wider. They are all around you.

In a sense, we can all find ourselves in that crowd. Sure, we've all been victims of people who've caused us pain. But we too have caused pain to others-- and, much more importantly, to God. With our words or our actions there have been times when all of us have denied and even cursed Christ. Yet he, again, determines to love us. Chooses to choose us. Even in the moments we are least lovable.

Of course Jesus was not finished. Three days later, he was seen alive again—making clear that he would continue to upend expectations rather dramatically. David's dynasty would be reestablished, but as a new kind of kingdom.

And *that* is how God's promise to David was ultimately fulfilled. His promise that the House of David would endure forever, a promise that seemed to have dried up like a dead olive branch, would slowly blossom into something more glorious than David––or that Palm Sunday crowd––ever dreamed. The Messiah would restore the kingdom not only by redeeming David's people, but by offering welcome and redemption even to those who would mock and oppose him. He distributes his lavish gifts of love to the completely undeserving.

When we ourselves receive that grace, when we are astounded that he loves even us, then the way we see others, even those who make our lives difficult, can completely change. We can see them through his eyes.

V
ALWAYS RELIABLE, RARELY PREDICTABLE

As I continue walking over the Mount of Olives down the Palm Sunday road, it occurs to me that the people who had cheered Jesus right here later became enraged partly because he would not fulfill their expectations of what the Messiah should do. They wanted him to kick out the Romans and establish a physical, earthly kingdom. This is what they had been praying for, faithfully and precisely, their whole lives. Their oppressors had been causing them pain, and they trusted God would deliver them. They were full of faith and expectation that God would send the

Messiah they longed for. All the while Jesus had something even more beautiful, freeing, and world-changing in mind.

And don't we all experience frustration with Jesus for precisely the same reason? We expect and pray for certain precise answers to prayer. We have faith and expectation God will move. But when he doesn't move in the ways we hope, we get frustrated. We may even turn on him, as the Palm Sunday crowd did. It's not that our faith is too small. It's that our imaginations are just not big enough.

God was totally faithful in fulfilling his covenant with David. Yet the way he fulfilled it was completely unexpected. And consequently many people missed the gift, because they were looking in another direction.

This is a truth about God I need to come back to whenever life seems unfair and painful. It feels like God is absent, allowing the bad guys to win. Didn't he promise to be my deliverer, to take care of me? But I can get *reliability* confused with *predictability*. God is *always* reliable. But almost *never* predictable.

You can't predict the way he will work...on any day.

But you can rely on him to work all things together for good...one day.

And you can absolutely rely on him to send good gifts... every day.

It's taxi driver wisdom for the ages. There may always be new drama swirling, new controversy making headlines, new tensions causing new fights, but God also keeps sending good gifts. They may not be the gifts you and I expect. But open your eyes a little wider. His gifts are all around you. His purposes soar far beyond the schemes of mere humans.

That's how you press on when people hurt you and insult you, when you feel betrayed and persecuted, when life isn't turning out as you'd hoped.

Remember what Jesus did for you, and all the others who stood mocking as he sacrificed his life on the cross. And remember to see his unexpected, unpredictable gifts as they blossom around you.

✧   ✧   ✧

Loping down the steep street toward Jerusalem on the Mount of Olives, I make a mental note. I really need to learn to pray that prayer of David, and the Son of David, every day. I think I've been clinging too tightly to my precise version of how God will work in my life. I need to release my grip and open my hands to receive whatever God has for me.

So I make a decision. Starting today, in this walk down the Mount of Olives, I will make their prayers, spoken on this very hill, a habit.

> *"If the LORD sees fit, he will...But let Him do as seems best to Him."*
>
> 2 SAMUEL 15:25,26 NLT

> *"Father, if you are willing, take this cup of suffering away from me. Nevertheless, your will, not my will be done."*
>
> LUKE 22:42 NLT

Then I get a pretty cool opportunity to start my new prayer habit.

As I near the bottom of the slope and approach the Kidron Valley, an opening looms in the tall rock wall to my left. A small sign declares this "The Garden of Gethsemane." Some olive trees here, the sign reads, are 2,000 years old. I turn into the garden, not yet crowded by tourists. I pause near the oldest, most gnarled tree, perhaps a witness to the moment the Son of David prayed this prayer. I bow my head, and make his prayer my own.

If you are willing...

Nevertheless, your will, not my will be done...

And I start to feel peace. ✧

DIGGING DEEPER

ABSALOM'S PILLAR

At the very bottom of the Kidron ravine separating the Mount of Olives from Jerusalem there's a massive ancient tomb nearly the height of a three-story building. For centuries people called this Absalom's Pillar, because the Bible says Absalom set up a monument—to himself!

Thanks to modern dating techniques, we now know this monument did not exist in Absalom's time. Absalom's actual pillar was probably destroyed centuries before Christ in one of the many wars here. However, what researchers discovered makes it even more interesting to me. It's the 2,000-year-old tomb of a wealthy man, possibly a priest.[5]

It was built a few years before the birth of Jesus, so it existed when he taught in this area. That makes this one of the tombs to which Jesus was referring when he said to the religious leaders, "You are like whitewashed tombs, which look beautiful on the outside but on the inside are full of the bones of the dead and everything unclean." (Matthew 23:27 NIV)

Sadly, that description matched David before Absalom's rebellion. He had the palace, but behind those walls, things were very unhealthy.

✳

EIGHT

FINDING PERSPECTIVE IN THE CHAOS

2 SAMUEL 21:15–17; 22:1–20

I

AN ANCIENT CHAMBER IN THE CITY OF DAVID

Finally I need to follow David to his death.

Today Danny and I are exploring the farthest reaches of the City of David, an area tour groups rarely venture. One of the most tantalizing discoveries in Jerusalem was made right here.

The possible tomb of King David himself.

Danny leads me clambering around the southeastern corner of the rocky hillside, where a lone security guard surveys the area from his tower. Danny gives him a friendly wave and then beckons me silently past some trees, out of sight of the guard. Oddly carved stone shapes loom out of the hillside. We walk through an ancient doorway cut into the rock and peer into a dark tunnel that stretches far into the hillside.

Danny explains what we're seeing. "The Bible says David was buried *in* the City of David. That's mentioned because it was so unusual; in Israelite culture, people were commonly buried outside city walls. So if David was buried within the ancient walls of Jerusalem at the time—which was a small, 14-acre site—there are only so many places his tomb could have been."

I'd read that the building on the other side of Jerusalem called "King David's Tomb" is almost certainly *not* the tomb of David; the structure there originated centuries after David, and isn't within the walls of the ancient city anyway.

"So is this the spot of his actual tomb?" I ask.

"Well," Danny says and grins, "The lead archaeologist here certainly thought so."

TALES FROM THE CRYPT

In 1913, Raymond Weill, a Jewish-French archaeologist, excavated tons of dirt and debris next to the hill here and found an old Roman-era quarry. Starting sometime after they defeated the Jewish rebels who led the Bar-Kokhba Revolt in 135 AD, the Romans began hacking limestone from this part of the ancient city for use in their nearby buildings. That explains the weird stone shapes. The Romans carved out only what they needed, leaving behind strange-looking limestone furrows and pits and arches.

But then Weill noticed something else. Apparently while expanding the quarry, the Romans shaved off the front facades of several massive ancient stone structures that had previously been carved into this hill. The interiors of these structures remain to this day, burrowing deep into the slope—eight elaborate manmade caves. The largest goes about 54 feet into the rock hillside. Weill identified these structures as tombs, and suggested that the largest, labeled "T1," may have been the royal tomb of the Davidic dynasty.

Not all archaeologists today agree with Weill's conclusions, but some influential scholars have recently revisited his ideas and found them compelling. Archaeologist Jeffrey Zorn, a Berkeley PhD and Cornell professor, argued in a 2012 journal article that other royal tombs from the same era in nearby cities match the style of these tunnels, and concludes "Weill's T1 and T2 are probably the remains of the tombs of the Davidic dynasty."[1]

We know David's tomb was still intact around 33 AD; that's when the Apostle Peter mentions it, as recorded in Acts 2:29. Josephus, writing shortly after 70 AD, writes of a failed attempt by King Herod earlier that century to break into David's tomb to rob it. But from 135 AD to 1173 AD, all record of the tomb vanishes from historical sources. The Romans likely defaced anything venerated by Jews as a royal tomb—they waged a systematic campaign to purge all traces of Jewish history from Jerusalem in the decades after the Bar Kokhba revolt.

Then one thousand years later, a medieval adventurer named Benjamin of Tudela wrote *The Book of Travels* describing his ten-year journey throughout the known world, from Northern Spain to Baghdad—and possibly further (he also writes about China and Ceylon, though his descriptions are sparse, perhaps accounts heard from other travelers). With surprising objectivity, he reports a story he heard in Jerusalem about the "miraculous" rediscovery of David's tomb in the Mount Zion area. He described the place still revered by many today as the Tomb of David, located on the other side of the Old City from the City of David location. But its historical value as the actual resting spot of David is in doubt; archaeologists say it's unlikely that there was Iron Age occupation there in David's era. That's why Weill, Zorn, and others support the hypothesis that the chamber labelled T1 is more likely to have been David's crypt.

VIEW FROM THE TOMB

Danny and I are standing at the entrance of T1. I look over at him. "Can we go inside?"

"Why not?" he shouts. He bounds into the cave, and I quickly follow.

After my eyes adjust to the lower light, I see something like a subway tunnel carved out of the grey rock, eight feet wide and twelve feet high, with a flat floor and rounded ceiling. At the back of the 54-foot long chamber is a deep ledge about six feet high. Danny scrambles up a precarious old wooden ladder to the ledge, but the ladder collapses under his weight just as he leaps to the rock shelf. I have to content myself with standing on tiptoe, peering up over the edge to see what's there. There's a shallow depression carved into the floor of the ledge. Danny walks it off to approximate a measurement: it's about six feet long and four feet wide, the perfect size for a human body—or casket.

After staring at what may have been David's final resting place, I turn around, toward the cave entrance, and see houses in the Arab village of Silwan across the ravine framed by the opening in the rock. The view reminds me of the day I began this journey, looking out of the shepherd's cave above the field of Boaz near Bethlehem.

I've gone from cave to cave. From birth to death.

I have a better understanding of David's era than I ever had before. But what I've been seeking is not just insight into his world. I've been seeking a way to understand the *point* of David. Why is his story given more space in the Bible than anyone else's—except for Jesus? Why all the drama, why all the detail about David's dark times and disastrous decisions? It's interesting, but what's the point, why is it there?

Before I draw my own conclusions, I wonder how David himself would answer that question. How would *David* have summarized the point of his life?

✧   ✧   ✧

Danny and I stroll out of the cave, down the old quarry, and across a lawn—part of the park that stretches across the eastern side of the City of David. I ask Danny for some time to myself. Now that my trip is coming to an end, I want to process what I've experienced. I reach into my backpack for my travel Bible and discover the Jerusalem bagel I'd squirreled away earlier that morning (no lie). I unwrap it and munch contentedly as I gaze into the distance. Then I remember: *The travel Bible! Oh yeah!*

Breaking the bagel's spell, I find my Bible, crack it open, and take a closer look at what may be the last thing David himself ever wrote. He gives us an x-ray of his soul at the end of a very rich, yet very rough life.

DIGGING DEEPER

STAR OF DAVID?

The six-sided Star of David (known as the *Magen David*, or "Shield of David" in Hebrew) is now the symbol most associated with David and Judaism. But it probably has no connection to the biblical David.

It was apparently first linked to David by non-Jewish alchemists and magicians in early medieval communities who called the six-pointed star the "Shield of David" and the five-pointed star the "Seal of Solomon." It wasn't until later that it appeared in Jewish manuscripts of the Bible as a meaningful symbol. In the 1600s, it began to be known in the Jewish community as a general sign of Judaism. In 1897 it was adopted as part of the Zionist flag by the First Zionist Congress.[2]

If the "Star of David" wasn't a symbol of Israel in ancient times, what was? The menorah, the palm branch, and the twin-pillared entrance to the Temple are often found in the remains of ancient Jewish homes and synagogues and served as the "Stars of David" of their era, symbols of the Jewish nation.

✻

WHEN THE TRIALS NEVER STOP

When David rides back into Jerusalem after Absalom's revolt, he's surely hoping for a time of peace. Instead there's another revolt almost instantly. Then a three-year drought. Then the Philistines start another war. Then David is almost killed.

It's a story most people don't know. David's cornered during a skirmish, a man with a raised spear is just about to murder him, and his nephew Abishai shows up at the last possible second and cuts down the enemy.

David is saved in the nick of time. But his closest advisors tell him, "You are *never* going out to battle again—it is too big a risk."

Imagine how hard that was for him to take. David the Giant-Killer. David the Great King. David the Legend. Now he's told, "You just don't have what it takes anymore." He was an old man and they were taking away the keys to the car. The way the Bible describes David in 2 Samuel 21:15 must have described his spirit in general at this point: *"He became weak and exhausted."*

AFTER ALL THESE YEARS

Right in this spot in the text—at this low point—the writer of Samuel inserts a song. Some scholars believe it may be the last psalm David ever wrote. It certainly sounds like an older, wiser man describing how he finds peace, even when life never seems to have gone quite the way he planned.

Look at these lyrics from the pen of a grizzled veteran of life's many battles:

> *The LORD is my rock, my fortress, and my savior;*
> *   my God is my rock, in whom I find protection.*
> *He is my shield, the power that saves me,*
> *   and my place of safety.*
> *He is my refuge, my savior...*
>
> 2 SAMUEL 22:2B–3 NLT

There's David's favorite way to think of God again: *fortress... refuge... place of safety*. Hideouts were a real thing in David's life. At this point he's had to bolt behind rocks and crawl into caves and seek sanctuary from sympathizers to escape his pursuers so many times he's probably lost count. But he knows the ultimate place of safety is God.

Fortresses fail and benefactors betray and caves fail to conceal—but God will keep his soul secure. No matter where David is physically, that oasis of safety is always available spiritually.

Need to find the way there yourself? Follow David. He's headed to the refuge in his next words.

Frame your past, present, and future as David did.

II
IN MY PAST: GOD HAS BEEN MY SAVIOR

David sees his own tumultuous past through a very interesting lens.

Think about what we've seen him face: prejudice, predators, giants, assassins, murderous kings, treacherous sons. There's the affair, the betrayal, the family feud. Then after Absalom's death, David returns to Jerusalem grieving his son, hoping for peace, and instead all hell breaks loose. Again.

How would you describe a life like that? Look closely at how David describes his past:

> I called on the LORD, who is worthy of praise,
>   and he saved me from my enemies.
> The waves of death overwhelmed me;
>   floods of destruction swept over me.
> The grave wrapped its ropes around me;
>   death laid a trap in my path.
> But in my distress I cried out to the LORD;
>   yes, I cried to my God for help.

He heard me from his sanctuary;
    my cry reached his ears.
He opened the heavens and came down;
    dark storm clouds were beneath his feet.
Mounted on a mighty angelic being, he flew,
    soaring on the wings of the wind.
He reached down from heaven and rescued me;
    he drew me out of deep waters.
He rescued me from my powerful enemies,
    from those who hated me and were too strong for me.

2 SAMUEL 22:4–7, 10–11, 17–18 NLT

You might read that and think, *Yeah, I'd love it if the heavens parted and I could see God show up like that.* But... when did *David* ever see that? He describes how God "opened the heavens and came down... mounted on a mighty angelic being... he reached down from heaven and rescued me." By now you've heard much of his story. So you know: *that never happened.*

David hid from Saul in caves and deserts—where was God then?

His own children turned against each other—where was God then?

He fled the city because of his son's betrayal—where was God then?

When you look back at David's story, you see that he actually never witnessed any kind of miraculous deliverance from his enemies. Nothing like the old stories he loved so much: no Passover angel smiting, no Red Sea parting, no Jericho walls tumbling. I think that's one of the reasons his story resonates so much with modern readers. David doesn't really see any miracles (except for a vision of an angel late in life, after this song). It's mostly just... life. With all its intense ups and downs.

So what is he talking about when he describes how God "reached down from heaven and rescued me?"

INVISIBLE. BUT THERE.

I think he's poetically expressing how, years later, looking back, he sees that God was powerfully active, even in those bleak days. God was invisible. But God was there. The whole time. For David, it's all God at work, whether God disguises himself with angel's wings or with Nathan's words, with the voice of thunder or with the voice of a friend.

I've heard older people reminisce about their tough times and remark, "It all seemed so dark then, but looking back, I can see God's hand was at work the entire time!" Remembering my own darkest moments—the deaths of my father and stepfather and mother, struggles with infertility and disease and anxiety—I can see God there too, bringing me to a better place, shaping my character, opening doors, "drawing me out of deep waters."

> God was invisible. But God was there.

I'm choking up a little even as I write, the memories evoking a flood of gratitude. Under this weird black cloud I've been under, it helps to recall the days the sun broke through. Gives me hope it's up there still, beyond the clouds, that it's just a matter of time before the gloomy morning overcast gets burned off by the warmth of a summer afternoon.

Reminiscing this way will do the same for you.

Here's why it's important to see the divine in the daily, God in the grit, angels in the everyday, as David does here. Sometimes we almost lust after miracles, for spectacular displays of God's power to blast away our troubles. And miracles do happen.

But there's a danger. In looking for the incredible, we can miss the incarnate.

Think of this: God was born into our ordinary lives as Jesus, into a feeding trough, among sheep and donkeys. No one stumbling onto that scene would have noticed anything miraculous. Just poor parents who found a pathetic substitute for a crib. But it was the greatest miracle ever.

And if you see your own life through David's eyes, you'll perceive how it was in common ways, through ordinary people, that God was coming down to help you. That friend bringing a meal? David would call that an angel soaring to help. That sunrise you saw on the way to work? The heavens opened. That song you heard just at the right time? God soaring to you on the wings of the wind, mounted on angelic beings, reaching down from heaven, pulling you out of deep waters.

David sees his crazy life, all the challenges he lived through, all the enemies and all the failures, and chooses to frame them not as an endless parade of difficulties, but as constant evidence of God's rescue.

So how are you narrating your own life? Are you always running the blooper reel, reminding yourself of all the ways you've messed up? Or do you look at the same exact years and run a highlight reel, reminding yourself of all the ways God blessed?

RESCUED

And did you notice the familiar emphasis for David in this verses? It's not about *his* effort, but about *God's* effort on his behalf. Look at the word he repeats:

*"He reached down from heaven and **rescued** me...*
*He **rescued** me from my powerful enemies*
   who hated me and who were too strong for me...
   *he **rescued** me because he delights in me."*

2 SAMUEL 22:17,18,20 NLT

He rescued me, he rescued me, he rescued me. They were *too strong for me.* But *God rescued me.* We often think of God as our coach, guru, advisor. But *rescue* implies complete helplessness. Drowning swimmers aren't coached. They are rescued. Patients flatlining on an operating room table aren't advised. They are rescued. Guilty sinners don't need a guru. They need a Savior. Even the great David admits that he had reached the end of himself, hit bottom, came to understand that he needed God. He needed God to *live.*

We seem to forget it, but this is the theme of the whole Bible. This is the gospel. What we could never do for ourselves, God has done for us.

This is the stunning opposite of what's often perceived as the Bible's message: *Try harder to be better so that God will like you more.* No, God does the rescuing.

THE DELIGHT OF GOD

And why would God rescue a helpless person like you and me? Read those wonderful words again: *"Because he delights in me!"*

Of course God's 100 percent *delight* doesn't mean God's 100 percent *approval.* Parents can take delight in their kids without approving their tantrums. Someone said good teachers fully embrace their students, no matter who they are... and then try to change them. That's a good description of how God works.

Embracing as is... and changing to be. God has unconditional love for you even as he develops you into maturity.

But the order is important. As Eugene Peterson says, "We don't first become good and then get God. First we get God—and then, over a patient lifetime, we're trained in God's ways."[3]

When you really start to believe God delights in you like that, then you begin

> God rescued us. Why? Simply because he delights in us!

delighting in God—and your spiritual growth takes off. Because now it's personal. You're not following rules issued from some cosmic CEO deity. You're in a relationship with a loving father.

III
IN MY PRESENT: GOD IS MY STRENGTH

Next David confidently asserts, "With your help I can attack an army. With God's help I can jump over a wall" (2 Samuel 22:30). What? Remember, this is right after his worst performance in a battle. He almost died! His physical prowess is gone. He's old. Weak. Yet watch how he describes what God does for him:

> *He makes me like a deer that does not stumble;*
> *he helps me stand on the steep mountains.*
> *He trains my hands for battle*
> *so my arms can bend a bronze bow.*
>
> 2 SAMUEL 22:34–35 EXB

Again, he is seeing reality through the eyes of a sanctified imagination. He's not saying he could outrun a young sprinter or outlift a young weight trainer. He's saying that God will give him all the strength he needs for the tasks he has left.

And God will help you stand, God will train your hands, God will strengthen your arms for the tasks you have left too.

BEND THE BRONZE BOW

The challenge in front of you right now may make you feel totally incapable—like someone being asked to bend a piece of metal with their bare hands. David's poetic imagery of bending a bronze bow means God will help you do what seems impossible. You can say with Paul: "I can do everything through Christ, who gives me strength" (Philippians 4:13 NLT).

Then David conjures one of my favorite images of grace:

> *You protect me with your saving shield.*
> *You have stooped to make me great.*
>
> 2 SAMUEL 22:36 EXB

You have stooped to make me great!

That's what God does. If he didn't, we could never reach him.

A thousand years after David, God stooped down from heaven to that manger in Bethlehem, the same village where David was born. And as Jesus grew, he kept stooping, stooping to touch lepers and sinners and other social rejects, to call them as he had called another reject a thousand years before, and then he stooped further still, all the way down into a grave. The story of Jesus is a stooping of majesty.

Why did he stoop to reach us? Just as David said, "to make me great." The New Testament tantalizingly insists that your rescue was accomplished not just to barely save you, not just to let you squeeze into heaven, not just to forgive your sins, but to transform you into a new creation. *To make you great!*

After all, why do you think God saved you? To make you sort of a mediocre sinner, never too far gone but never really triumphant either? To make you into a fine inoffensive church-goer? No, he rescued you for *greatness*.

> God has stooped to make me great.

It may not look like the greatness our society rewards. But he is perfecting something great in you. You can be great at compassion, great at peacemaking, great at joy. As a pastor I've spoken at many funerals. I've noticed that this is the kind of greatness that gets remembered by friends and loved ones, long after all the other supposedly great accomplishments fade. This is the kind of greatness that changes the world in all the ways it really needs changing.

Say it with confidence. *"God saved me to make me great."* Try it now.

"God saved me to make me great!"

If you're unsure about the truth of that, read these words:

*Even before he made the world, God loved us and chose us in Christ to be holy and without fault in his eyes... For we are God's **masterpiece**. He has created us anew in Christ Jesus, so we can do the good things he planned for us long ago.*

EPHESIANS 1:4; 2:10 NLT, EMPHASIS MINE

DIGGING DEEPER

A GATE TO DAVID'S TIME

In June 2019 archaeologists revealed that they had unearthed a city gate from the time of David in the ancient city of Bethsaida. One of the unusual features of this discovery: it was found in northern Israel, on the Golan Heights.

Until this discovery, physical evidence of structures dating to David's era had been rare this far north. The discovery was so unexpected that archaeologists from all around the world were called in to carefully sift and document the site. Professor Rami Arav of the University of Nebraska, chief archaeologist overseeing the excavations, told the Jerusalem Post that they are now cautiously identifying the city as the biblical Zer, named in Joshua 19:35 as one of the Canaanite fortified cities that Joshua allotted to the Israelite tribe of Naphtali.[3]

The city gate found in the ruins was built centuries after Joshua's era, as part of an expansion around the time of David. A carved monument dedicated to a local lunar deity was found near the gate, leading some to theorize that the city was occupied in the 10th Century B.C. by the small kingdom of Geshur, and may have been fortified as a response to David's rising influence from the south.

✳

IV
IN MY FUTURE: GOD IS MY SECURITY

Finally David bursts with confidence as he looks ahead despite his constant sorrows:

You give great victories to your king;
you show unfailing love to your anointed,
to David and all his descendants forever.

2 SAMUEL 22:51 NLT

Unfailing love.

After all these years, all his triumphs and all his failures, David still believes God calls him *beloved.*

The elderly David keeps remembering God's goodness:

Is it not my family God has chosen?
Yes, he has made an everlasting covenant with me.
His agreement is arranged and guaranteed in every detail.

2 SAMUEL 23:5 NLT

In this moment of physical weakness, when the reality of aging hits him hard, when a wrinkled, worn-out David is benched, pitied, no longer allowed on the field, forced into semi-retirement, he still believes with all his heart that God does not love him any less than when as an agile young boy he struck down a giant. Because he believes his worth is not dependent on his performance. It's based on a covenant guaranteed by God. Forever.

As Danny returns and we stroll back through Jerusalem, I ask him if he ever feels a sense of wonder anymore about living here in Israel. This journey has been amazing for me, but is it still awe-inspiring for a resident, particularly an academic?

"Well," he says, "There is something that can't help but inspire wonder as you see all these layers of civilization. The Edomites, the Moabites, the Philistines, the Phoenicians, they all disappeared. Only the Jews lasted. The question should really be, not just why did those other cultures disappear, but how did the Jews survive all the atrocities and challenges they faced?"

I can't stop thinking about his observation. None of the people groups of David's world are intact today, none of the languages of David's world are commonly spoken today, none of the religions of David's world are being followed today, none of the sacred texts of David's world are venerated today—except for David's.

How is that even possible? I know how King David would explain that mystery.

God established a covenant.

He made a promise to David—and we are still seeing the effects of that promise today. The Jewish people have indeed outlived nations far stronger and more firmly entrenched, from the Assyrians to the Babylonians to the Romans.

But acknowledging the power of God's covenant means more than just living in wonder at the continued existence of the Jews. The survival of David's people means I have reason—actual, living evidence—to trust that through all of life's challenges and changes, all the puzzles and problems, all the ups and downs, God is sovereign. That same covenant that gave David hope 3,000 years ago can give me hope that he will sustain me through all my trials—and will revive and restore his kingdom through the Son of David.

V

HOW YOU FRAME IT CHANGES HOW YOU FEEL IT

Look again at the ways David framed his past, present, and future in this, his last great song. Do you recognize it? David has come full circle. He emphasizes the exact three things he proclaimed in 1 Samuel 17, his very first moment on the public stage:

> God has saved me in the past.
> *"The LORD who rescued me from the claws of the lion and the bear will rescue me from this Philistine!"*
>
> 1 SAMUEL 17:37 NLT

> God will give me the strength I need for the present.
> *"...it is not by sword or spear that the LORD saves; for the battle is the LORD's."*
>
> 1 SAMUEL 17:47B NIV

> God has a future for me and His people.
> *"...everyone assembled here will know that the LORD rescues his people."*
>
> 1 SAMUEL 17:47A NLT

That's how David frames his life. From start to finish.

So much of your joy comes down to this: *How do you frame your life?* Do you see it as a parade of pointless circumstance? A string of bad luck? Proof that others have it good while you have always struggled? Evidence of your oafishness—or your genius?

Or do you see it as repeated proof of God meeting you at your point of greatest need, as a chain of events that may start as bummers but end as blessings? Choose your frame carefully.

✵ ✵ ✵

I'll never forget asking my mother, when she was in the middle stages of her Alzheimer's disease, what lesson she had learned from life. I hoped to hear some words of wisdom before the *aphasia*, the symptom of her illness that made it difficult for her to express her thoughts, rendered her permanently unable to communicate.

What a life: She had endured World War II in Europe. She'd lost her first husband, my father Fred, to cancer when my sister and I were toddlers. She lost her second husband, Jet, to a heart attack when we were college-aged. Years of poverty followed in her widowhood, plus a fire and a flood that devastated her possessions, and many more tragedies.

> So much of your happiness and joy come down to this: *How do you frame your life?*

So I asked the question. What have you learned through all that?

She stopped and stared into the middle distance for a long time. At first I thought that she hadn't been able to understand me. Then she turned back to me, held my hands in hers, locked eyes with mine. I watched her face as she fought hard past her illness. And she spoke four words, very slowly, very deliberately, very firmly.

"*The. Lord. Will. Provide.*"

Her grip got tighter and her stare more intense as she said it again. This woman—who was forgetting so much—desperately wanted me to always remember this.

"The! Lord! Will! Provide!"

A smile creased her face. We both cried. And embraced. As it turned out, that was almost literally her last word on life. Not, *Man, I've had it tough.* But *The Lord will provide.* Because that's exactly what she'd seen. Tough times, yes. But also God giving her just what she needed at just the right time in just the right way. God riding in on the wings of angels, swooping in from the heavens, rescuing her from powerful enemies.

> The Lord will provide.

That's how she framed it. So that's how she felt it.

I mentioned earlier how the pagan stories of old always end in tragedy. That's the way those ancient cultures framed life.

No matter how hard you try, the gods will get you.

The Bible stories offer a totally different paradigm.

No matter how hard life is, God's got you.

THE HERO OF EVERY STORY

As I read my Bible on the slopes of the City of David I suddenly see the point David is making in this song—and the point to his whole story in the Bible.

The hero of the story is not David. It's God.

The mistake I've made in the past is trying to see David as a heroic example of moral behavior. That gets confusing, because although he's a successful soldier and reasonable ruler, he fails pretty miserably at a lot of other important stuff.

David is not a *hero*; David is *us*. David is an ultra-high-def picture of what people are like. Not *supposed* to be like. Just *are* like. He is far from the *ideal* human. But he is sort of the *classic* human, one who lived all the ups and all the downs, all the inconsistencies, all the mistakes, and all the triumphs that a person could have, at full intensity. He is the Bible's archetype of a person in covenant relationship with God. Very flawed. Yet chosen as an iconic vessel of God's grace, so that God can be glorified.

> When bad things happen to you and when you do bad things, God still loves you.

I think David's in the Bible to show what it's *really like* to be in a relationship with God. Not what it's like to be in some imagined, ideal relationship, but a real relationship, to love and question and argue and complain and fight and leave and rebel and return—and yet never be unloved.

Now, at the end of my quest, I see that all through his story, someone keeps chasing David. And never lets up.

It's not Saul. It's not any of his enemies.

It's God.

He keeps chasing David wherever he wanders, into the valleys and caves and throne rooms and bedrooms, always eager to call him home.

And he's chasing you too.

WHERE THE BAD THINGS ARE

I read in a recent survey that people are most likely to leave the faith when they hit tough times, or when they have a recurring habit or sin in their lives they feel is inconsistent with following Christ. In other words, when bad things happen to them, or when they do bad things, that's when they tend to bail.

Why? Maybe they think God doesn't love them anymore. Maybe they don't feel worthy. Maybe they wonder if those bad things mean the absence of God.

But David's life shows that even when bad things happen to you (as they happened to him, a lot) and even when you do bad things (as he did, a lot) God still loves you. Still chooses you. Still is with you. Where the bad things are.

Martyn Lloyd-Jones said it this way:

> *How can I put it plainly? It doesn't matter if you have almost entered into the depths of hell. It does not matter if you are guilty of murder as well as every other vile sin. It does not matter from the standpoint of being justified before God at all. You are no more hopeless than the most moral and respectable person in the world.*[5]

That's what David's story shows, in sometimes uncomfortable detail. In his life, theological concepts like grace and redemption and adoption aren't abstractions; they become organic, personal, specific. Awkward, messy, wonderful. Outrageous, beautiful, incarnate. God's grace is not meant to stay neat and pretty on the pages of a textbook. It's for real life, for real people. Like David. And like you.

WHO'S ON YOUR LIST?

This beautiful truth in David's story—that God uses ordinary, flawed people— is in the Bible not just to change your internal narrative about yourself. This is also about changing the way you see others.

His own family voted young David *Least Likely to be Used by God*—yet God used him in amazing ways. So who do you overlook, who do you ignore, who do you dislike and disqualify? Who would you not invite to the gathering if someone showed up to choose God's next great leader? You probably think of yourself as very tolerant. But be honest. Who are the people you size up and write off?

The redneck with the gun rack on his pickup? The activist with a peace sign on his VW? The gutter-dweller, the mansion-dweller, the young know-it-all, the retired know-it-all, the blue-haired, the blue-tattooed, the cross-dresser, the croissant-eater, the alcoholic, the teetotaler, the progressive, the conservative, the poor, the rich, the immigrant, the WASP? The ones who called you names in school, the ones who hurt you so bad you still have scars, the ones who lied to you, laughed at you, yelled at you, the ones who litter the beach, talk in movies, cut in line, the ones who flip you off, cut you off, tick you off? God loves them all, offers grace to them all, has a destiny for them all. None are perfect. All are absolutely, totally, infinitely, unconditionally beloved.

> God loves to choose the least likely suspects to be objects of his grace and agents of his purpose.

Does that make you uncomfortable? Think again of David. God's grace blasted into David's life in ways so outrageous—God was so generous and so forgiving—that it seems kind of... unfair. In fact, if you don't feel a little uncomfortable with the lavish way God ladled love and blessing on David, you just haven't been paying attention.

I'd say it's *supposed* to make you uncomfortable, supposed to make you think. Because David's life shows you how God works.

He loves to choose the least likely suspects to be objects of his grace and agents of his purpose.

I like Eugene Peterson's observation:

There's no moral or spiritual symmetry between God and David; it's totally lopsided on the side of God. Unknown David is named and known. Unequipped David is triumphant. Undefended David finds refuge. Undeserving David is forgiven. Unworthy David recovers his kingship. The David story is a gospel story, God doing for David what David could never do for himself. A sinner saved.[6]

And that is how understanding David's story helps you understand every other story in the Bible. The hero in any of these stories is never the Bible character. *The hero is always God*, who keeps choosing misfits, keeps changing destinies, and keeps wiping sins away.

David's story is really not finished until we get to the Jesus story. There, in the flesh, we see clearly what God is like, what David poetically imagined God doing in his final song, what God has always been doing and always will do: saving, stooping, seeking the undeserving, the unhealthy, the unholy. And redeeming them.

BELIEVING IN REDEMPTION

This is important because we are in a cultural moment when everyone's quick to write off those who fall or offend in any way. Mercy is not exactly trending right now.

I get it. People, especially in positions of authority, have gotten away with a lot. The time for accountability is long overdue. There should be consequences for bad behavior. At the same time, we need to be careful not to fall into a simplistic, reductionistic, legalistic way of sizing others up that leaves no room for second chances. Yes, people sin. A lot. But God loves redemption. It's kind of his thing. He takes flawed people, including whoever's on your list as the worst on the planet, and transforms them with his grace. And by the way, you are probably on someone else's list.

Think of the people Jesus personally selected as his disciples. In their inconsistency and thick-headedness and amazing potential, they remind me so much of David. As Frederick Buechner observes:

> *Jesus made his church out of human beings with more or less the same mixture of cowardice and guts, of intelligence and stupidity, of selfishness and generosity, of openness of heart and sheer cussedness as you would be apt to find in any of us. The reason he made his church out of human beings is that human beings were all there was to make it out of. In fact, as far as I know, human beings are all there is to make it out of still. It's a point worth remembering.*[7]

Yes. Remember that. Remember it about them and about David and about you.

Like David, you will have successes and failures, you will be truly amazing and you will be really awful. Sometimes people will anoint you as the next best thing and sometimes people will disrespect you as the old useless thing.

When any of that happens, don't let *self-pity* get the best of you and don't let *pride* get the best of you.

Instead, keep circling back to the grace of God. Believe in the possibility of redemption for you and everyone else. He *still* has a plan for you... because He still delights in you.

But does he really delight in me still, you may be thinking, *after all I've done?*

God proved it a thousand years after David, right in David's city. When I stood in what may have been David's tomb, it struck me that the Son of David didn't wait for Romans to hack away at the entrance to *his* tomb. God blew it apart, blasting away the stone that sealed it, raising Christ from the dead.

> Keep circling back to the grace of God.

And when Jesus stepped out of his grave, he chased down those misfits he had chosen—even though they had abandoned him, denied him, cursed him—with an offer of reconciliation. *Do you love me?* He asked. *Then get back in the game.*

That same Jesus is chasing you down. As Brennan Manning put it,

> ...*Jesus Christ, who this moment comes right to your seat and says, "I have a word for you. I know your whole life's story. I know every skeleton in your closet. I know every moment of sin, shame, dishonesty and degraded love that has darkened your past. Right now I know your shallow faith, your feeble prayer life, your inconsistent discipleship; and my word is this: I dare you to <u>trust</u> that I love you just as you are and not as you should be."*[8]

CONTINUING THE JOURNEY

As our jet lifts off from the Tel Aviv airport, I look out the window at sort of a God's-eye-view of Israel and think back on my experience chasing David all around the countryside there.

And I see that David's God was chasing me the entire time. He has been teaching me something, in every location. In fact, it was the same thing. Over and over.

He rescued me because he delights in me.

An irony is becoming clear to me. I say I believe in God's grace for my salvation. And I do. I preach about it all the time in my church. I've been writing about it in this book.

But I slowly realize I've been *living* like someone without the daily reassurance of God's delight, constantly telling myself, *You're not good enough, you're not pure enough, you're not accomplished enough.* I haven't been grounding my day-to-day self-perception in grace; I've been basing it on my performance. Which will always disappoint.

I need to realize that God knew about all my flaws when he chose me. Before I was even born, he knew I'd be a son and student and husband and father and friend and pastor and neighbor, and he already knew then all the ways I'd screw up those things later. That doesn't give me an excuse to keep screwing up (because David's life also models for us the potentially far-reaching consequences of our behavior). But it does remind me to lean away from trust in my inconsistent self and to lean into the delight-giver, the covenant-maker, the sin-forgiver.

✣ ✣ ✣

I'm headed home. But will you continue this journey with me? It's a journey in a new direction, away from a focus on your own failures. Or your successes. It's a turning from a focus on yourself at all. It's about losing yourself in adoration of the God who chased you down until he found you—found you overlooked, facing giants, hiding in a cave; found you fallen from a roof, run out of town, benched from the game; found you old, exhausted, tired. And he rescued you. Because he delights in you.

You'll fall again, you'll forget again, you'll fear again.

But when you do, don't berate yourself for not being perfect. And don't make excuses for yourself either. Just turn as soon as you can to the God who chose you and still chooses you, who gave a destiny to you and has a destiny for you still, who delighted in you while you were in your mother's womb, fresh as a Jerusalem bagel, and still delights in high-mileage you.

There's no question. After all these years, he still calls you "Beloved." As Max Lucado puts it, "The question is, do you call him Savior?"[9]

When you turn back toward him, you'll be on a familiar trail. Look around. There's David walking beside you, weeping over his mistakes but weeping even more with joy at the outrageous generosity of the God who keeps choosing him. There too are all those disciples, those cowards and doubters and naysayers, and you can see on their faces that they are awestruck that Jesus keeps choosing them too.

And as your vision clears you'll see someone else with you on the path. Someone who's always been with you. It's the risen Christ, walking with you and David and all his other very human and very flawed and very beloved friends, all the way to the New Jerusalem, where, at last, the long-awaited Son of David reigns as king forever. ✴

ENDNOTES

PROLOGUE

1. *Selections from the Book of Psalms* (New York: Grove Press, 1999), x.

2. Abram Leon Sachar, *A History of the Jews*, (New York: Alfred A. Knopf: 1967), 34.

3. Jonathan Kirsch, *King David: The Real Life of the Man Who Ruled Israel* (New York: Random House, 2000), 372.

4. *...it's the David/Jesus story.* This is a great term for the Bible coined by Eugene Peterson in *Leap Over a Wall: Earthy Spirituality for Everyday Christians* (New York: HarperCollins, 1997), 10.

5. Margreet Steiner, "It's Not There: Archaeology Proves a Negative." *Biblical Archaeology Review* 24, no. 4 (1998): 26ff.

6. "'David' Found at Dan," *Biblical Archaeology Review* 20, no.2 (1994): 26.

7. "The Tel Dan Inscription: The First Historical Evidence of King David from the Bible," *Biblical Archeological Review*, May 2, 2019, https://www.biblicalarchaeology.org/daily/biblical-artifacts/the-tel-dan-inscription-the-first-historical-evidence-of-the-king-david-bible-story/0 (accessed on April 29, 2019).

8. J.I. Baker, ed., "Walt Disney: From Mickey to the Magic Kingdom," New York: *LIFE Books* 16, no. 3 (April 15, 2016): 49.

9. André Lemaire, "House of David Restored in Moabite Inscription," *Biblical Archaeology Review* 20, no. 3 (1994): 30–31.

CHAPTER ONE
FINDING CONFIDENCE WHEN REJECTED

1. Evan Andrews, "Who Were the Sea Peoples," History.com, June 2, 2017, https://www.history.com/news/who-were-the-sea-peoples (accessed June 6, 2019).

2. Gino Dimuro, "Who The Sea Peoples Were And How They Devastated The Ancient World," ATI.com, June 26, 2018, https://allthatsinteresting.com/sea-peoples (accessed June 6, 2019).

3. Simon Worrall, "The Little Town of Bethlehem Has a Surprising History," National Geographic.com, Dec. 23, 2017, https://news.nationalgeographic.com/2017/12/bethlehem-christ-birth-blincoe/ (accessed on May 9, 2019).

4. Phillippe Bohstrom, "Vast 4,200-Year-Old Prehistoric Necropolis Found by Bethlehem," *Haaretz*, March 6, 2016, final edition (accessed on May 24, 2019).

5. Sandra L. Richter, *The Epic of Eden* (Downer's Grove: IVP Academic, 2008), 201.

6. From transcript of speech presented by Brennan Manning at the Omni Hotel Atlanta July 8, 2007 For Alive Communications' Authors and Industry Executives © Brennan Manning, 2007

7. Goodreads.com, https://www.goodreads.com/author/quotes/7810781.D_Martyn_Lloyd_Jones (accessed on May 23, 2019).

8. David Seamands, *Healing for Damaged Emotions Workbook* (Colorado Springs: David C. Cook, 2004), 190.

9. Brennan Manning, *The Ragamuffin Gospel* (Colorado Springs: Multnomah, 1990), 14.

10. Amanda Borschel-Dan, "Israeli scientists brew groundbreaking 'ancient beer' from 5,000-year-old yeast," *The Times of Israel*, May 22, 2019, final edition, (accessed on May 30, 2019).

CHAPTER TWO
FINDING COURAGE TO FACE GIANTS

1. For much more on this fascinating discovery, read this book by the archaeologists themselves: Garfinkel, Ganor, and Hasel, *In The Footsteps of King David* (London: Thames & Hudson, 2018).

2. "Ancient DNA sheds light on the origins of the Biblical Philistines"

3. https://www.sciencedaily.com/releases/2019/07/190703150509.htm (accessed July 8, 2019).

4. Michael S. Heiser, "Clash of the Manuscripts: Goliath & the Hebrew Text of the Old Testament," BibleStudyMagazine.com http://www.biblestudymagazine.com/extras-1/2014/10/31/clash-of-the-manuscripts-goliath-the-hebrew-text-of-the-old-testament (accessed May 14, 2019).

5. Tim Collins, "Roman sling bullets used against Scottish tribes 2,000 years ago were as deadly as a .44 Magnum," Daily Mail Online, May 25, 2017 www.dailymail.co.uk/sciencetech/article-4541318/Roman-sling-bullets-deadly-44-Magnum.html (accessed April 3, 2019).

6. Heather Pringle, "Ancient slingshot was deadly as a 44 magnum," National Geograpic.com, May 24, 2017, https://news.nationalgeographic.com/2017/05/ancient-slingshot-lethal-44-magnum-scotland/ (accessed April 3, 2019).

CHAPTER THREE
FINDING LIGHT IN THE DARKNESS

1. Abigail Klein Leichman, "Escape the Heat in Israel's Top 10 Caves," Israel 21C.com, June 25, 2012, https://www.israel21c.org/top-10-caves-of-israel/ (accessed on May 30, 2019).

2. Charles R. Swindoll, *David: Man of Passion and Destiny* (Dallas: Word, 1997), 74.

3. Michel Quoist, Prayers (New York: Sheed & Ward, 1963), 138.

4. Taylor Clark, "It's Not the Job Market: The three real reasons why Americans are more anxious than ever before," Slate.com, January 31, 2011, slate.com/culture/2011/01/american-anxiety-the-three-real-reasons-why-we-are-more-stressed-than-ever-before.html (accessed on June 13, 2019).

5. Vaclev Havel quoted in David Brooks, *The Second Mountain: The Quest for a Moral Life* (New York: Random House, 2019), 206.

6. Adapted from John Wheeler, "King David's Harp," HarpSpectrum.org, www.harpspectrum.org (accessed on April 3, 2019).

CHAPTER FOUR
FINDING POWER TO FORGIVE

1. Thomas L. Friedman, "Plunging Into the Judean Desert," *The New York Times*, March 16, 1986, final edition (accessed on May 24, 2019).

2. Barlow, Wrosch, Gouin and Kunzmann, "Is Anger, but Not Sadness, Associated With Chronic Inflammation and Illness in Older Adulthood?" *Psychology and Aging* 34, no. 3 (2019) 330–340.

3. Tim Herrera, "Let Go of Your Grudges. They're Doing You No Good," *The New York Times*, May 19, 2019, final edition, (accessed on June 13, 2019).

4. Adapted from Daniel E. Miller, *When Others Make Your Life Difficult* (Berlin, OH: TGS International, 2016), 54–55.

5. Manning, 90.

CHAPTER FIVE
FINDING HOPE WHEN DREAMS DIE

1. Eilat Mazar, *Excavations at the Summit of the City of David, Preliminary Report of Seasons 2005–2007*, (Jerusalem and New York: Shoham, 2009), 52.

2. Eilat Mazar, "Did I Find King David's Palace?" *Biblical Archaeology Review* 32, no. 1 (2006), 16–18.

3. Kirsch, 115–117.

4. Erez Ben-Yosef, "Beyond smelting: New insights on Iron Age (10th c. BCE) metalworkers community from excavations at a gatehouse and associated livestock pens in Timna, Israel," *Journal of Archaeological Science: Reports*, 11 (February 2017), 411–426 (Online version accessed July 8, 2019)

5. https://news.nationalgeographic.com/2017/03/king-solomon-mines-bible-timna-dung/ (accessed on July 8, 2019)

6. Richter, 107.

7. Shukron explains his findings on video at www.youtube.com/watch?v=_ EKaN6FXwVw (accessed on May 30, 2019).

CHAPTER SIX
FINDING GRACE WHEN YOU FALL

1. Michael B. Sauter and Charles Stockdale, "The most dangerous jobs in the US include electricians, firefighters and police officers," US Today, January 8, 2019, final edition (accessed on May 24, 2019).

2. Kirsch, 201.

3. *Hidden Brain* podcast, National Public Radio, June 14, 2019, (accessed June 14, 2019).

4. Rolf Dobelli, *The Art of Thinking Clearly* (New York: Harper, 2014), 184.

5. Peterson, 183.

6. "Jeremiah's Opponents," sidebar to Eilat Mazar, "The Wall That Nehemiah Built," *Biblical Archaeology Review*, March–April 2009, https://www.baslibrary. org/biblical-archaeology-review/35/2/21 (accessed on May 1, 2019).

7. Hebrew University Press Release, https://m.phys.org/news/2015-12-israelite-judean-king-exposed-situ.html (accessed June 29, 2019)

CHAPTER SEVEN
FINDING STRENGTH WHEN PEOPLE CAUSE YOU PAIN

1. Miller, 37–38.
2. Avraham Faust and Yair Sapir, "The 'Governor's Residency' at Tel 'Eton, The United Monarchy, and the Impact of the Old-House Effect on Large-Scale Archaeological Reconstructions", *Radiocarbon*, 60, no. 3 (June 2018), 801–820, DOI: https://doi.org/10.1017/RDC.2018.10 (accessed on June 19, 2019).

3. https://www.breakingisraelnews.com/106811/new-archaeological-find-confirms-sophisticated-davidic-kingdom/ (accessed on June 19, 2019).

4. Ibid.

5. "The Tomb of Absalom – First Century Jerusalem," BibleHistoryOnline.com www.bible-history.com/jerusalem/firstcenturyjerusalem_tomb_of_absalom. html (accessed on May 24, 2019).

CHAPTER EIGHT
FINDING PERSPECTIVE IN THE CHAOS

1. Jeffrey R. Zorn, "Is It David's Tomb?," *Biblical Archaeology Review* 38, no. 6 (2012): 44–52, 78.

2. https://www.britannica.com/topic/Star-of-David accessed on April 29, 2019

3. Peterson, 216.

4. https://www.jpost.com/Israel-News/Archaeologists-discover-city-gate-from-time-of-King-David-591653 (accessed on June 26, 2019)

5. Goodreads.com https://www.goodreads.com/author/quotes/7810781.D_Martyn_Lloyd_Jones (accessed on May 23, 2019).

6. Peterson, 211.

7. Frederick Buechner, *Secrets in the Dark*, (New York: HarperSanFrancisco, 2006), 147.

8. Brennan Manning quoted in Ed Cyzewski, *A Christian Survival Guide: A Lifeline to Faith and Growth* (Grand Rapids: Kregel, 2014), 193.

9. Max Lucado, *Facing Your Giants* (Nashville: Thomas Nelson, 2006), 180.

MEMORY VERSES

1. FINDING CONFIDENCE WHEN REJECTED

People look at the outward appearance, but the LORD looks at the heart.

1 SAMUEL 16:7 NIV

2. FINDING COURAGE TO FACE GIANTS

It is not by sword or spear that the LORD saves; for the battle is the LORD's.

1 SAMUEL 17:47B NIV

3. FINDING LIGHT IN THE DARKNESS

I will take refuge in the shadow of your wings until the disaster has passed.

PSALM 57:1 NIV

4. FINDING POWER TO FORGIVE

Refrain from anger and turn from wrath; do not fret— it leads only to evil.

PSALM 37:8

5. FINDING HOPE WHEN DREAMS DIE

You, Sovereign LORD, have spoken, and with your blessing the house of your servant will be blessed forever.

2 SAMUEL 7:29 NIV

6. FINDING GRACE WHEN YOU FALL

Have mercy on me, O God, because of your unfailing love. Because of your great compassion, blot out the stain of my sins.

PSALM 51:1 NLT

7. FINDING STRENGTH WHEN PEOPLE CAUSE YOU PAIN

Let all that I am wait quietly before God, for my hope is in him. He alone is my rock and my salvation, my fortress where I will not be shaken.

PSALM 62:5,6 NLT

8. FINDING PERSPECTIVE IN THE CHAOS

He led me to a place of safety; he rescued me because he delights in me.

2 SAMUEL 22:20 NLT

DISCUSSION
GUIDE

NOTE

These questions are meant only as a guide. Use them as tools to evoke productive discussion. Don't feel pressure to finish all the questions. In fact, you may be inspired to write new questions based on your own group's needs. Of course, try to stay on topic and avoid divisive discussions veering into politics or other topics that may be distracting from the group's purpose.

CHAPTER ONE
FINDING CONFIDENCE WHEN REJECTED

TOUCH BASE 15–20 MINUTES

As you kick off your group, have each group member share their name, and how long they've lived in the area.

What are you looking forward to most in this study?

Take a moment to draw a picture in each of the two squares below (it's okay if it doesn't look perfect; stick figures are fine, as long as you can tell what it is!). These are pictures of two things from your childhood that formed you significantly. They could be good things or hard things, or both! Give your group five minutes to draw, then have each person share what they drew and why.

Today we take a look at the most significant event in the early life of King David.

TAKE IT IN 12 MINUTES
Watch the video for "Chasing David Week 1" on DVD, on YouTube®, or at tlc.org/david.

Video Notes:

TALK IT OUT 25–35 MINUTES

1. Why do you think David is such an intriguing Bible character, even though he is very flawed?

2. When you were young, did you ever feel left out, made fun of, or unskilled? If you're comfortable, share a little about that.

3. Have someone in your group read 1 Samuel 16:1–7. Why do you think Samuel initially thought Eliab was the Lord's anointed?

4. When you hear that God "looks at the heart" instead of the appearance, does this comfort you—or alarm you?

5. Apparently David was not even invited to the gathering when Samuel came to anoint one of Jesse's sons. What does that suggest about his position in the family?

6. Have someone in your group read what David wrote in Psalm 139:13–16. In what ways does David describe his "chosenness" in these verses?

7. Read 1 Corinthians 1:26–29. How do the Apostle Paul's words emphasize the same truths we've seen in this lesson?

8. Throughout his life, David keeps returning to this moment again and again—the moment he was chosen by God and made aware of his destiny. Would you say you live with a sense of God choosing you, loving you, and giving you a destiny? Why or why not?

9. René wrote, "…our 'chosenness' does not mean a life free from struggle." How would a belief that "I am truly chosen and loved by God" make a difference when going through tough times?

10. What do you honestly believe God thinks of you at this very moment? How does that compare to the verses you read today?

TAKE IT HOME 10 MINUTES

How can you advocate for the weak, overlooked, needy, or disqualified? How could your group participate in a project to help such people?

CLOSE IN PRAYER

CHAPTER TWO
FINDING COURAGE TO FACE GIANTS

TOUCH BASE 10 MINUTES

Today we look at the story of David and Goliath. What Goliath—a giant problem or fear or challenge—are you facing right now?

TAKE IT IN 12 MINUTES

Watch the video for "Chasing David Week 2" on DVD, on YouTube, or at tlc.org/david.

Video Notes:

TALK IT OUT 25–35 MINUTES

1. What stood out to you from this week's lesson (from the video, sermon, or book)?

2. Read 1 Samuel 17:33–37. David found courage when facing the giant by remembering how the Lord had helped him in the past with lions or bears. What "lion or bear" have you confronted in the past—a giant difficulty or problem—that the Lord has helped you defeat?

3. Read 1 Samuel 17:45. Why didn't David feel small when facing such a massive opponent?

4. Do you tend to spend more time thinking about the Goliath who taunts you—or the God who strengthens you?

5. How can you increase your God-thoughts and decrease your Goliath-thoughts?

6. David kept returning to his identity as someone God has specifically chosen and blessed with a destiny. Read Ephesians 1:3–14. It's okay if you don't understand every single word in this passage; for now, just list all the things God did for you, according to these verses.

7. How can truly believing these things help you face the Goliaths in your own life?

8. After David killed Goliath, "...then the men of Israel and Judah surged forward with a shout and pursued the Philistines" (1 Samuel 17:52 NIV). It was after David defeated a giant that the others were finally inspired to fight and win. Have you been inspired by seeing the victory of others over a "giant?"

TAKE IT HOME 10 MINUTES
In 1 Samuel 17:47 David said, "The battle is the LORD's." In what specific situation will you remind yourself of this truth this week?

Who do you know facing a giant right now? How could you encourage them? How could your group encourage and help someone facing a giant?

CLOSE IN PRAYER

CHAPTER THREE
FINDING LIGHT IN THE DARKNESS

TOUCH BASE 10 MINUTES

Today we join David in the darkness. Describe which of these it feels like in your life right now, and why:

> The middle of the night
>
> Just before dawn
>
> Sunrise
>
> Middle of the day
>
> Sunset

TAKE IT IN 12 MINUTES

Watch the video for "Chasing David Week 3" on DVD, on YouTube, or at tlc.org/david.

Video Notes:

TALK IT OUT 25–35 MINUTES

1. What stood out to you from this week's lesson (thoughts from the video or sermon, passages in the book)?

2. As René said, the Bible contains two Psalms David wrote during his cave time. Have someone in your group read one of them, Psalm 142, aloud. How would you describe this prayer of David to the Lord?

3. Why is realizing my powerlessness an important step to getting strength from God?

4. Have someone read Psalm 57, another of David's "cave psalms" aloud. What phrase or thought jumps out at you from this passage—is there imagery David uses that you like, or a phrase that intrigues or surprises or comforts you?

5. Many of the Psalms in the Bible are not "happy"—they are laments about how terrible life is going. Why do you think they are included in the Bible, and not just happy songs?

6. C.S. Lewis wrote that the solution to low self-esteem and low morale "...is not to think *more* of myself, and the solution is not to think *less of myself*; the solution is to think of myself less." Do you agree? Why or why not? How can you actually do that?

7. Have someone read Romans 8:28–39. How do these verses in Romans 8 give hope and comfort for cave times?

8. René wrote, "What truly forged David into a king was actually not any of the seemingly promising events that happened before his cave time. It was in the stink and squalor and sadness of the cave that David starts his true trajectory to the throne. In exile he is forged into the leader he is meant to be. And it's in our caves that you and I are made into the people God wants us to be." Do you agree or disagree with this? Why? Have you seen this happen your life? How?

TAKE IT HOME 10 MINUTES
Think of ways you or your group might help some "cave dwellers"—people who are desperate, embittered, indebted.

CLOSE IN PRAYER

CHAPTER FOUR
FINDING POWER TO FORGIVE

TOUCH BASE 10 MINUTES

As the group starts, have any members share if they have been able to put insights from this study into practice in real life:how about overcoming criticism or facing giants or surviving cave times?

Today we look at how David forgives Saul. Is forgiveness easy or hard for you?

TAKE IT IN 12 MINUTES

Watch the video for "Chasing David Week 4" on DVD, on YouTube®, or at tlc.org/david.

Video Notes:

TALK IT OUT 25–35 MINUTES

1. Read the exciting story in 1 Samuel 24:1–15. Why do you think David was able to restrain himself from taking vengeance on Saul? How do you honestly think you would have have responded?

2. Max Lucado wrote in his book about David, *Facing Your Giants*, "Vengeance fixes your attention on life's ugliest moments...freezes your stare at cruel events in your past. Is this where you want to look? Will rehearsing and reliving your hurts make you a better person? By no means. It will

destroy you." Do you agree? Why or why not? How have you seen this to be true in your own life?

3. Have someone read David's words in Psalm 37:1–11 aloud. What helpful phrases or truths or perspectives jump out at you from these verses?

4. Where are you struggling to "be still" and "wait patiently" on God right now?

5. Read Romans 12:14–21.
   Why are believers not supposed to take revenge, according to Romans 12:19?
   Instead, what are we supposed to do, according to Romans 12:20–21?
   Have you ever seen kindness change someone's enemy? How so?

6. René wrote, "There is a difference between grace and gullibility. There is a difference between forgiveness and trust. You *have* to forgive people. The Bible commands it. You *don't* have to trust them. Forgiveness, by definition, is *given*. It is not earned or deserved. Trust *must* be earned." Do you agree that this is an important distinction? Why or why not?

7. If you are willing, share with the group how you have learned to show grace to someone in your life who caused you grief. How did God work in your life to get you to that point? What have you learned?

8. If you are willing, share a time that you were forgiven by someone. Each one of us has also been forgiven so much by God. How would a focus on how you've been forgiven help you in your forgiveness of others?

TAKE IT HOME 10 MINUTES

We all have people in our lives that are hard to forgive. What's the next right step you can take to treat those people in your life with grace?

CLOSE IN PRAYER

CHAPTER FIVE
FINDING HOPE WHEN DREAMS DIE

TOUCH BASE 10 MINUTES

Today we look at a time God said "no" to David's dream. Share with your group how you have been able to apply the lessons of this study so far—perhaps in forgiving someone or facing fear with courage.

TAKE IT IN 10 MINUTES

Watch the video for "Chasing David Week 5" on DVD, on YouTube®, or at tlc.org/david.

Video Notes:

TALK IT OUT 25–35 MINUTES

1. Has God ever said "no" to a dream of yours... and now, looking back, you're glad he did? What happened?

2. Read 2 Samuel 7:1–11. Does God seem at all bothered that he does not have a temple?

3. What does the Lord want David to understand about their relationship (verses 8,9)? What do you find comforting in the way God told David "no"?

4. Read 2 Samuel 7:12–17. What are the things God promises David?

5. Read 2 Samuel 7:18–29. What is David's response to God's "no?" In what ways do you think this prayer is a model for how to respond when God says no?

6. René wrote: "David prays, ...with your blessing... your servant will be blessed. This is one of the most essential yet most elusive choices you and I can make: choose to be blessed with God's blessing." Do you agree or disagree? Why is it sometimes hard to pray, "with your blessing I will be blessed?"

7. Is gratitude to God for his blessings easy or difficult for you? Have you found ways to improve your gratitude?

8. Have a group member read this section:

Paul the Apostle had travel plans in Acts 16. He wanted to go into Asia Minor. But God said no. Instead, God directed Paul to Europe, where the growth of Christianity exploded. God's "no" led to a better "yes." Paul the Apostle also had what he called "a thorn in the flesh," apparently some sort of physical weakness. He prayed for God to take it away, but God said no. Why? Read these verses from 2 Corinthians 12:8,9:

"Three different times I begged the Lord to take it away. Each time he said, 'My grace is all you need. My power works best in weakness.' So now I am glad to boast about my weaknesses, so that the power of Christ can work through me." (NLT)

What reason for God's "no" does Paul receive here? What do you think this means?

9. René wrote: "We can't know the cosmic purpose for every single heartache. We can know this: *God will never waste a hurt.* He will work through all the pain to bring growth and new life." How have you seen this to be true in your life?

DEEP DIVE

If you have the time, take this deep dive. Have a group member read this section out loud:

2 Samuel 7 contains some of the most important verses in the Bible, both in Jewish and Christian tradition. They are usually referred to as "the Davidic Covenant," the first major covenant (or agreement) between God and humans since Moses—and the last until the new covenant is fulfilled in Christ. In a sense, these verses are the theological climax of the entire Old Testament to this point, and they are quoted and paraphrased many times in the rest of the Bible.

In the Davidic Covenant, God specifically promises that a great king would come one day with these characteristics:

- He will be a descendant of David (verse 12)
- "He shall build a house for my name..." (verse 13)
- God will "...establish the throne of his kingdom forever." (verse 13)
- God says "I will be to him a father, and he shall be to me a son." (verse 14)

These promises were imperfectly fulfilled in Solomon, David's son. But the biblical prophets later recognized that they would be perfectly fulfilled one day in a future descendant of David. Here is just a sample of what they prophesied:

> *"The days are coming," declares the LORD, "when I will raise up for David a righteous Branch, a King who will reign wisely and do what is right and just in the land. In his days Judah will be saved and Israel will live in safety. This is the name by which he will be called: The LORD Our Righteous Savior."*
>
> JEREMIAH 23:5,6 NIV

> *For to us a child is born, to us a son is given, and the government will be on his shoulders. And he will be called Wonderful Counselor, Mighty God, Everlasting Father, Prince of Peace. Of the greatness of his government and peace there will be no end. He will reign on David's throne and over his kingdom... from that time on and forever*
>
> ISAIAH 9:6,7 NIV

By the time of Christ, people were enthusiastically anticipating this "Messiah." Yet in ways they never expected, Jesus a fulfillment of this promise to David!

In other words, God's *no* to David led to a much better *yes* for all of humanity!

How does this encourage you?

TAKE IT HOME 10 MINUTES

What steps can you take this week to redirect your thoughts towards God's goodness in the midst of a "no?"

CLOSE IN PRAYER

CHAPTER SIX
FINDING GRACE WHEN YOU FALL

TOUCH BASE 10 MINUTES

Are you ever surprised at your own actions—particularly when you act in a way you know you shouldn't? What's one example?

TAKE IT IN 10 MINUTES

Watch the video for "Chasing David week 6" on DVD, on YouTube®, or at tlc.org/david.

Video Notes:

TALK IT OUT 25–35 MINUTES

1. Read 2 Samuel 12:1–7. Why do you think Nathan dealt with David's sin by telling him a story first?

2. Why do you think this story about David is in the Bible? Why is it so important to remember both the consequences of self-destructive behavior *and* the steps to recovery?

3. Read what David wrote about this episode in Psalm 32:3–5. Our decision to sin can literally have physical consequences. How does David say he felt during the time he tried to cover up his misdeed? How did God respond when David finally confessed?

4. Read one of David's famous masterpieces, Psalm 51, written about this chapter in his life. What turns of phrase or ideas jump out at you from this psalm as interesting or revealing?

5. In verse 12, David writes, "Restore to me the joy of your salvation, and make me willing to obey you." David requests two things that seem to be linked: joy... and a willingness to obey. René wrote: "If all I feel when I think of God is condemnation, then I am not going to want to be near Him. But if I find *joy* there, I will *want* to follow Him."

    Do you agree? How has this played out in your own spiritual life history?

6. René wrote: "Stop thinking that if you only feel guilty enough, you'll stop...Guilt is not enough to motivate change. Get help. And keep getting help."

Why is it so hard to actually take action and get help for our sins, addictions, and destructive habits? Can you share encouragement about a time you sought help and it changed you in a positive way?

7. René wrote: "The Bible says, just as God chose David, he chose you. And he will never *unchoose* you. He has a future for you. He does not want you to be chained to past mistakes and regrets. In fact, He made an astounding sacrifice on a cross... precisely to slice those chains off."
   How do you honestly respond to that paragraph: Do you believe it? Does it seem too good to be true? Is it difficult to believe?

8. Read Ephesians 2:1–10. What truths do you see in these verses about both our sinfulness and God's grace? How does this encourage you?

9. Where in your life story are you seeing (or have you seen) God redeem your failures?

TAKE IT HOME 10 MINUTES

No matter what path you have taken, God can redeem you. And no matter where you are in your relationship with God, none of us is immune to a moral failure. What one thing will you take home from this story to help you in your walk this week?

CLOSE IN PRAYER

CHAPTER SEVEN
FINDING STRENGTH WHEN PEOPLE CAUSE PAIN

TOUCH BASE 10 MINUTES

In your family of origin, how was loved primarily expressed: Through words, acts of service, physical hugs, gifts, quality time, or another way?

Can you describe a positive influence your mom, dad or other parental figure had on you?

TAKE IT IN 10 MINUTES

Watch the video for "Chasing David week 7" on DVD, on YouTube®, or at tlc.org/david.

Video Notes:

TALK IT OUT 25–35 MINUTES

1. As René wrote in the book, this is a tough section of the Bible to take in. The consequences of bad behavior by David and others are intense and heart-breaking. When David hears what Amnon did to Tamar, he is very angry—yet he does not seek justice and in fact tries to keep the situation quiet. How do you think David should have handled Amnon's crime?

2. David has a strange relationship with his son Absalom: he clearly loves his son, and yet for years he won't even talk to him. Of course this causes problems. What does this story say to you about parenting—and relationships in general?

3. Many years later, David (and the entire kingdom) bore the negative consequences that grew out of David's refusal to seek justice for Tamar: for one thing, his son Absalom became so angry that he tried to overthrow David, causing a war. Does this story say anything to you about the long-term consequences of ignoring injustice?

Note: As always, David's story shows *consequences* of bad behavior... and *recovery* from bad behavior, too.

4. Many believe Psalm 62 was written during this season in David's life. He is on the run again at age 60, this time chased out not by Saul but by his son. This is a psalm about keeping perspective when life is full of problems—even if you caused some of the problems yourself. Have someone read Psalm 62 while the rest of the group follows along. What words or turns of phrase from this psalm jump out at you, or intrigue you?

5. Read 2 Corinthians 4:8–9,16–18. Very little in the Apostle Paul's ministry went as he planned, but what attitude does he demonstrate in these verses?

6. Read Genesis 50:20 and Romans 8:28. These verses are essentially an Old Testament and New Testament version of the same promise. How would you summarize it?

7. Share a tough time in your own life when the belief that God was in control provided you with comfort.

TAKE IT HOME 10 MINUTES
What's one principle from this week's lesson that you will apply to a specific situation this week?

CLOSE IN PRAYER

CHAPTER EIGHT
FINDING PERSPECTIVE IN THE CHAOS

TOUCH BASE 10 MINUTES

In today's verses, David looks back on a life filled with hills and valleys—and finds perspective.

Looking back on your own life, are there some low times—some deep valleys—that you view a little differently now, with better perspective?

If you were asked to write one sentence summarizing what you've learned or experienced in life, what would you say?

TAKE IT IN 10 MINUTES

Watch the video for "Chasing David week 8" on DVD, on YouTube®, or at tlc.org/david.

Video Notes:

TALK IT OUT 25–35 MINUTES

1. David said, "God rescued me because he delights in me" (2 Samuel 22:20 NLT). Is it hard for you to believe God delights in you? Why or why not?

2. Read 2 Samuel 22:1–20. David describes God's intervention in his life with dramatic words! Yet he never literally saw God acting like this in his life—riding down from heaven with blasts of heat and lightning, for example. What do you

think is David's point here? Is there a principle that applies to your own life?

3. David's song is divided into three sections. Share some of the ways you have seen God act in these same three ways in your own life:

> *In my past God has been my Savior*
> How has God rescued you, provided for you?

> *In my present God is my strength*
> How are you seeing God strengthen you now?

> *For my future God gives me security*
> What gives you comfort as you look ahead?

4. Why is it so important to talk regularly—to others and yourself— about what God has done for you?

5. Have someone in your group read the very last psalm of David included in the Bible, Psalm 145. In verse 8, David quotes a verse written about 400 years before David, when Moses wrote that the Lord appeared to him and told him these words:

> *"The LORD is gracious and merciful, slow to anger and abounding in steadfast love."*
>
> **PSALM 145:8**

This is actually the Bible verse most quoted by the Bible itself! How is this different from the way many people see God? How is Psalm 145:8 a fitting recap of David's own life?

6. How do you think it would impact your life if you truly believed that verse, to the core of your being, every day?

TAKE IT HOME 10 MINUTES

As we wrap up our look at the life of David, what is a life lesson that you will take away from this study?

CLOSE IN PRAYER

THANK YOU

THANKS ARE DUE TO SO MANY PEOPLE WHO HELPED WITH THIS BOOK

The knowledgeable and energetic Danny Herman (check out his web site: dannythedigger.com). I amused myself by taking some artistic license with my descriptions of Danny's driving. He's really a very safe driver and an inexpressibly great guide! Also major thanks to our other wonderful guides in Israel, including the very witty and creative Michel Kahn, who has led two groups from Twin Lakes Church with me and I hope will lead many more, and our two Bethlehem-area guides Sana and Johnny. The Bethlehem guide of chapter 1 named Sara was a composite: 99%

was Sana, and other 1% was the person who kept pointing out the seeds in my teeth. Enormous gratitude and credit is due to our talented project photographer, videographer, and producer Jamie Rom; my wife Laurie who helped so much with book edits and was our "key grip" on site; Valerie Webb, who shepherded the project to completion; Valerie, Jim Josselyn, and Dave Hicks, who helped with the study guide questions; and Karen O'Connor, Sherri Kyle, Neil Pearlberg, and Mark Spurlock, who all gave me wonderful suggestions for the manuscript. Karen, Andrew Summers, and Faye Malone are proofreading angels and any remaining errors are mine alon. I mean, mine alone. Thanks also to our graphics team including Jennifer Boudreau, who drew the book maps, and the amazing crew at Seven Roots Creative, including Murphy Felton, Angie Sterrett, Josh Bootz, and others, who designed the cover, did the layout, and contributed in many other ways.

I'm especially grateful to the people in the wonderful congregation I serve, Twin Lakes Church in Aptos, who provide me the time and encouragement to do these projects, and for Gary Gaddini and Steve Clifford, amazingly uplifting pastors who dared me to make this material available to other churches.

Most of all I am grateful to the Son of David, Jesus, for his many blessings and continual grace and patience with me. ✿

Notes

Notes

Notes

Notes

Notes

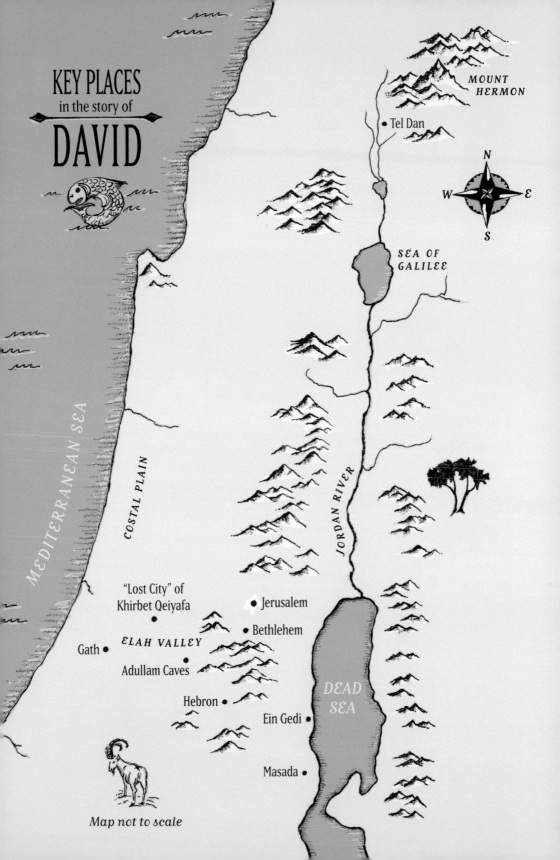

KEY PLACES
in the story of
DAVID

MOUNT
HERMON

• Tel Dan

N
W   E
S

SEA OF
GALILEE

MEDITERRANEAN SEA

COSTAL PLAIN

JORDAN RIVER

"Lost City" of
Khirbet Qeiyafa
•

• Jerusalem

• Bethlehem

ELAH VALLEY

Gath •

Adullam Caves

DEAD
SEA

Hebron •

Ein Gedi •

Masada •

Map not to scale

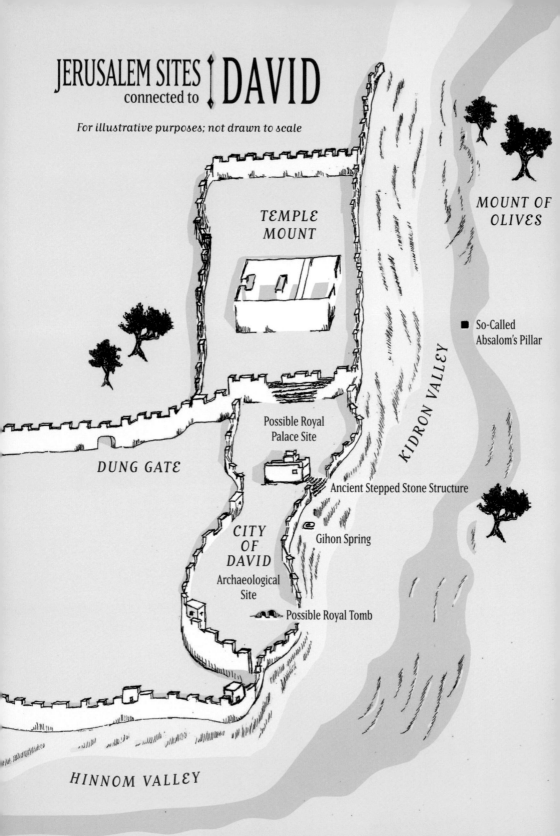

JERUSALEM SITES
connected to DAVID

For illustrative purposes; not drawn to scale

TEMPLE MOUNT

MOUNT OF OLIVES

So-Called Absalom's Pillar

KIDRON VALLEY

Possible Royal Palace Site

DUNG GATE

Ancient Stepped Stone Structure

Gihon Spring

CITY OF DAVID
Archaeological Site

Possible Royal Tomb

HINNOM VALLEY

Tel Dan, where the famous Tel Dan Inscription was found in 1993—the first known mention of David and his empire in an ancient document outside the Bible.

The Tel Dan inscription, which contains the most ancient reference to "The House of David" yet discovered outside the Bible

Irresistible Jerusalem bagels

Suburbs of modern Bethlehem surround the traditional Field of Boaz, once owned by David's great-grandfather.

The ruins of Khirbet Qeiyafa near the Elah Valley. This 3,000-year-old Israelite city was lost for centuries until archaeologists finished uncovering it in 2013. They believe it demonstrates the rapid sophistication of Israel under the United Monarchy of David and Solomon, confirming the general picture painted in the Bible.

The cliffs of Israel are dotted with thousands of caves—so many that most are not on any maps. That made this area an ideal place for early humans to find shelter, and for fugitives like David and his men to find hideouts.

The Ein Gedi ravines are an oasis in the Dead Sea wilderness, providing water, shelter, and food for birds, animals... and exiles like David.

The author peering into one of the many caves and tunnels in the Ein Gedi area. They provide naturally air-conditioned refuge from the desert heat, offer convenient boltholes to escape pursuers—and can even serve as private bathrooms. Or so Saul thought.

Teddy-bear-like hyraxes love to nap on tree branches throughout the Ein Gedi oasis.

Charles Warren's archaeological team in Jerusalem. Warren would be the first to suggest that King David's Jerusalem lay buried under a forgotten Palestinian Arab neighborhood, not in the walled Old City. He unearthed a series of tunnels that would later lead to major discoveries. (Photo credit: By Elliott & Fry—extantamericana, Public Domain, https://commons.wikimedia.org/w/index.php?curid=14965236)

Part of the ancient "Large Stone Structure" found by archaeologist Eilat Mazar under a modern building on the City of David hill in Jerusalem. She suspects it was the administrative center of ancient Jerusalem, including David's palace.

Another part of the extensive Large Stone Structure, with a facsimile of the Phoenician column piece found by Kathleen Kenyon. Discovered just below this hill, Dr. Mazar considered it a clue to the location of David's palace.

Ruins of the Stepped Stone Structure, a massive series of terraces and retaining walls that reinforced the hill below the royal palace in ancient Jerusalem. Archaeologists have found homes of wealthy families built into this structure. They would have enjoyed beautiful views and privacy—unless the king happened to catch someone bathing on a rooftop.

The path from the Mount of Olives through the Kidron Valley toward the Temple Mount and, just around the corner, the City of David. The so-called Absalom's Pillar, a tomb with a conical roof, is near the center. Although named for David's son Absalom, this structure dates instead to the time of Christ, and was probably a tomb for a wealthy priest.

The entrance to T1, the chamber in the City of David some archaeologists believe may have served as the royal tomb of the Davidic dynasty. In the Roman era the front section of this cavern was hacked away, removing forever valuable clues to its original purpose.

The author and his archaeologist guide Danny Herman.

The Dead Sea is beautiful, but its waters are useless for quenching thirst—in fact, they can kill you.